P9-CFB-430

VGM Opportunities Series

OPPORTUNITIES IN **FORENSIC SCIENCE CAREERS**

Blythe Camenson

Foreword by
Anita Hufft, Ph.D., R.N.
Professor and Associate Dean for Academic Programs
Louisiana State University School of Nursing

Library of Congress Cataloging-in-Publication Data

Camenson, Blythe.
Opportunities in forensic science careers / Blythe Camenson.
p. cm. — (VGM opportunities series)
ISBN 0-658-00101-9 (hardcover)
ISBN 0-658-00102-7 (paperback)
1. Forensic sciences—Vocational guidance. 2. Criminal investigation—Vocational guidance. I. Title. II. Series.

HV8073 .C316 2001
363.25'023'73—dc21

00-66817

Published by VGM Career Books
A division of The McGraw-Hill Companies.
4255 West Touhy Avenue, Lincolnwood (Chicago), Illinois 60712-1975 U.S.A.

Printed in the United States of America
International Standard Book Number: 0-658-00101-9 (hardcover)
0-658-00102-7 (paperback)

2 3 4 5 6 7 8 9 0 LB/LB 0 9 8 7 6 5 4 3 2

CONTENTS

ABOUT THE AUTHOR

Blythe Camenson is a full-time writer with more than four dozen books to her credit, most on the subject of various careers. She is the coauthor of *Your Novel Proposal: From Creation to Contract* (Writer's Digest Books) and director of Fiction Writer's Connection, a membership organization for new writers, which you can find at www.fictionwriters.com.

FOREWORD

As early as A.D. 700 the Chinese used fingerprints to establish the identity of documents and clay sculptures, although they did so without any formal classification system. It was Quintilian, an attorney in the Roman courts, who in about A.D. 1000 showed that bloody palm prints had been used to frame a blind man of his mother's murder. As you can see, the beginnings of forensic science are ancient, and those interested in pursuing forensic science as a career follow in very old footsteps.

Modern forensic science, also known as *criminalistics*, has been a career dedicated to the identification and evaluation of evidence related to criminal investigation since the nineteenth century, when, in 1880, Faulds and Herschel first described the uniqueness and permanence of fingerprints. Simply put, forensic science is the application of science to the law. And there are many applications.

Opportunities to establish a career in the forensic sciences have never been as diverse or accessible as they are today. Never before has there been the opportunity for education, technology, social services, and political action to come together so comprehensively to address criminal activity. Although the violent crime rate declined 10 percent in 1999—reaching the lowest level in the history of National Crime Victimization Survey data—and the property crime rate declined 9 percent—continuing a more than twenty-year decline—violence, victimization, and crime continue to be a significant social and health concern of the United States.

Those interested in a career in forensic sciences are wise to consider as many resources as possible to acquaint themselves with the possibilities of linking their own skills and interests to the workforce needs in such diverse fields as forensic medicine, forensic archaeology, forensic anthropology, forensic computer sciences, and forensic nursing.

Forensic science uses widely varied and highly sophisticated technologies to discover and analyze evidence in a number of different fields. The most common application of forensic science is in the investigation of criminal activities such as assault, robbery, rape, or murder, but it is also used in the civil courts system, in monitoring food and drug safety and environmental indicators, and to test for the presence of chemical and nuclear weapons.

In the pages to come you are invited to learn more about specific fields in forensic science and to take what is offered in this text to explore career opportunities in private and public service, to interview those working in the field, and to look for needs in which creating new forensic science applications may be appropriate. It is an exciting and growing specialty in which the scientist can provide unique and important contributions to the legal processes that serve society.

Anita Hufft, Ph.D., R.N.
Professor and Associate Dean for Academic Programs
Louisiana State University School of Nursing
New Orleans

ACKNOWLEDGMENTS

The author would like to thank the following professionals for providing information and advice on careers in the forensic sciences:

A. Midori Albert, Forensic Anthropologist
Jan Bailey, Psychiatric Technician
William Foote, Forensic Psychologist
Robert Lemons, Fire Investigator
Sandra Ramsey Lines, Forensic Document Examiner
Jack Murray, Accident Investigator
George Reis, Forensic Digital Imaging Consultant
Randy Skelton, Forensic Anthropologist
Patricia Speck, Forensic Nurse
Douglas Ubelaker, Forensic Anthropologist

CHAPTER 1

FORENSIC SCIENCE FIELDS

Law and Order, LA Law, NYPD Blue, Quincy, The Practice, Family Law, The X-Files, and scores of other TV programs over the years have brought into our homes the concept of forensics. Even the O.J. Simpson trial, which played out in our living rooms like a television serial, made "DNA," "bloody gloves," and "footprints" household words.

Police and attorneys order the study of crime scenes and appoint experts to collect and examine evidence—fingerprints, hairs, fabric fibers, footprints, and so on. The end result often can bring participants to a court of law, where guilt or innocence can be decided. And it's the court of law where the term "forensic" is most often applied.

The word "forensic" is derived from the Latin word *forensis,* which means "of the forum." The forum is where the law courts of ancient Rome were held. With that in mind, it makes sense that today's definition of "forensic" refers to the application of scientific principles and practices to the legal process, during which expert testimony often plays a role. In other words, "forensic" (an adjective) means pertaining to, connected with, or used in courts of law.

Forensic science is the acquisition and analysis of scientific data for application to the study and resolution of crime, investigation, civil and regulatory issues, and criminal identification.

THE ROLE FORENSIC SCIENTISTS PLAY

The forensic sciences play an important part in our justice system. Although most of its disciplines have become identified primarily with law enforcement because of television and movies, this is misleading. Forensic scientists may be involved in all aspects of a criminal case, and the results of their work may help either the prosecution or the defense. The point of forensic science is to use all the scientific information available to determine facts.

Although mostly associated with criminal proceedings, forensic science comes into play in an increasingly active role in the civil justice system as well. Questions of law and fact may require forensic science expertise for a number of reasons. A forensic scientist can attest to the validity of a signature on a document—a contract or a will, for example—or can judge if a corporation is complying with terms of a liability settlement.

Because of forensic science, the number of cases entering the overloaded court system can be reduced. Reports produced by forensic scientists can show if a case has merit and should actually go to court.

Forensic science also has been helping to restore the faith people once had in our legal system. The belief that the legal process results in justice has been shaken over the last few years. Now, with DNA technology and advances in other related areas, the forensic scientist can help present the facts in a criminal or civil case, without depending on circumstantial evidence or unreliable witness testimony.

Although the gathering and examination of forensic evidence plays probably the largest role, there is much more to forensics than just DNA matching.

FORENSIC SCIENCE FIELDS

For further clarification, let's look at the different types of evidence as well as the definitions for other specific fields. The chapter where further discussion can be found is noted after each topic.

Forensic evidence. Scientists and experts (also known as criminalists) work in the following areas:

Computer and digital image enhancement

Crime scene reconstruction

DNA
Documents
Drugs
Entomology
Fingerprints
Firearms-ballistics
Footwear and shoeprints
Hair fibers
Handwriting
Linguistics/audio
Locks
Paint
Photography
Poisons and other toxins
Polygraphs
Sculpting
Voice and speech analysis
Tire tracks and skid marks
Toolmarks (Chapter 2)

Forensic accident investigation: Experts reconstruct accidents for testimony in law cases (Chapter 3).

Forensic pathology: Pathology is the study of disease. Forensic pathology requires additional training and is the application of the principles of pathology, and of medicine in general, to legal issues. Forensic pathologists perform autopsies and conduct other investigations (Chapter 4).

Forensic coroners or forensic death (medical or legal) investigators: Those who gather evidence and/or conduct autopsies or other investigations for information to be used in the court system (Chapter 4).

Forensic medicine: the application of medical knowledge to questions of civil and criminal law, especially in court proceedings (Chapter 4).

Forensic odontology: Forensic odontology is a branch of dentistry that deals with the collection, evaluation, and proper handling of dental evidence to assist in civil and criminal proceedings (Chapter 4).

Forensic nursing: Forensic nurses work in both crime scene investigations and in areas such as rape crisis centers. They often work with forensic social workers (Chapter 4).

Forensic anthropologists, artists, and sculptors: Those who use their expertise to create reconstructions that can help identify remains or assailants (Chapter 5).

Forensic psychology and psychiatry: The application of the related professions of psychology and psychiatry to questions and issues pertaining to law and the legal system. Scientists in this area can help determine if a suspect is competent to stand trial or if he or she knew the difference between right and wrong when committing a crime (Chapter 6).

Forensic social workers, psychiatric technicians, mental health workers, and counselors: Those who work with offenders involved within the criminal justice system (Chapter 6).

OTHER FORENSIC DISCIPLINES

In addition to the established specialties mentioned above, there are many new areas of forensic study that are just emerging:

Forensic Computer Examination: Forensic computer experts prove fraud or other crimes in which computers are involved. Some experts specialize in forensic accounting, investigating and interpreting bankruptcies, and other complex financial transactions. Using accounting techniques they attempt to determine the patterns of people who might have committed frauds.

Forensic Accounting: Forensic accountants study white-collar crime such as fraud, embezzlement, or tax evasion.

Forensic Economics: Forensic economists estimate the value of the victim's present and future lost income resulting from wrongful injury or death.

Wildlife Forensics: Wildlife forensic scientists work in two main areas: identifying evidence, and linking the suspects, victims, and the crime scene by means of physical evidence. They determine poaching violations and work with state and federal officials to develop hunting regulations. They also are concerned with the Endangered Species Act.

Wildlife forensics differ from criminal science only in that the victim (and occasionally the perpetrator) is an animal.

Forensic Engineering: Forensic engineers put their expertise to work in legal-related matters, such as the quality evaluation of construction or manufacturing, failure analysis, and maintenance procedures. The role of the forensic engineer also can overlap with accident and arson investigators. Structures forensic engineers examine can range from apartment buildings or bridges to surgical implants or bones. Their expertise is applied in personal injury cases; construction, contract, or warranty disputes; patent or copyright infringements; and criminal and regulatory matters.

Forensic engineering is a specialized practice of the engineering sciences, not a separate discipline. Few universities offer courses in forensic engineering; therefore, forensic engineers must develop their own credentials. Most perform their services part-time in addition to other work, such as college teaching.

Forensic Architecture: Forensic architects investigate construction defects and code violations for evidence to be used in a court of law. Their role can sometimes overlap the role of the forensic engineer. There are also other forensic specializations, such as forensic administration, research, rehabilitation, laboratory investigation, field investigation, communications, and forensic education.

THE ROLE OF LAWYERS

Law is at the core of forensic sciences, and lawyers work hand in hand with forensic scientists, advancing the search for truth.

To be fully effective, a forensics specialist not only must be an expert in his or her discipline, but also must be expert in communicating findings in legal proceedings. No matter how accurate the findings are, if a forensic specialist can't communicate results in a clear fashion to the law firm that hired him or her or to a jury in a court of law, his or her abilities are useless.

A forensics specialist also must be familiar with and conform to the laws governing collection, preservation, and admissibility of evidence. If an investigation is tainted, a case can be lost—or won.

Lawyers who use expert testimony in their work should have a better than basic knowledge of all the forensic sciences and must be articulate in presenting the findings of the expert witness. No matter how qualified the expert witness may be, and however accurate the analysis of the evidence, the value of these tests and analyses will be diminished if the lawyer is untrained in the field and is unprepared to present the evidence effectively.

SAMPLE JOB TITLES

Forensic scientist positions come with a variety of job titles. Some employers might designate entry-level jobs with Roman numerals, for example, Forensic Scientist I or Forensic Pathologist II. Other titles include (but are not limited to):

Administrator of public services
Assistant medical examiner
Chemist
Criminalist
Deputy medical examiner
Director of laboratories
Document examiner
Drug chemist
Firearms examiner
Forensic chemist
Forensic consultant

Forensic DNA analyst
Forensic drug analyst associate
Forensic pathologist
Forensic scientist
Forensic scientist (DNA/trace evidence)
Forensic technologist
Histologist
Latent fingerprint examiner
Medical examiner
Odontologist
Professor (assistant, associate, or full)
Tool mark examiner
Toxicologist
Trace analyst
Trace evidence technologist

JOB SETTINGS

Forensic scientists are employed by federal, state, and local governments and agencies. Some work for private laboratories; others work for universities. Still others work in hospitals and clinics or in private practice.

Self-employed forensic specialists might work in accident reconstruction or offer digital image-enhancing technology. The range of settings is as wide as the range of specialties.

SAMPLE JOBS

The following administrative listings are provided as a sample only, and as such, the hiring firms are not mentioned. You may look for current listings by doing an Internet search using keywords such as "jobs" and "forensics."

Additional sample jobs are provided throughout the book.

Administrator-Public Services 2 (Police/Crime Lab)

The City of ______, Department of Police Operations—Crime Lab is seeking applicants for the position of Administrator-Public Services 2. Qualifications include a bachelor's degree in chemistry, biology, physics, forensics, or criminalistics that included course work in general chemistry, organic chemistry, instrumental analysis, quantitative analysis, and physics; and six years of responsible experience in a forensic laboratory of which two years must have been in a supervisory capacity. Must be court qualified in at least two fields of forensics.

Responsibilities include planning, coordinating, and supervising the work and staff of the crime laboratory, and preparing reports for and testifying as an expert witness in hearings and in court as required. Salary: $55,671–$65,491.

Director of Laboratories

The ______ County Health Department is seeking applicants for the position of Director of Laboratories to oversee a full-service crime laboratory (criminalistics, forensic biology/DNA, and toxicology). Qualifications include a Ph.D. in toxicology, biology, chemistry, and/or forensic science or a directly related field; thorough knowledge of modern laboratory techniques in toxicology and/or the forensic sciences; and a minimum of five years of laboratory bench work experience in one of the forensic disciplines as well as three years of laboratory administrative experience. ABC or DBFT board certification is desirable. Salary: $93,777–$100,670.

Forensic Administrator

The ______ County Regional Forensic Science Center is seeking applicants for the position of Forensic Administrator. Qualifications include a bachelor's degree in business, administration, or management with a background in forensic science. Responsibilities include managing the daily operations of the facility and supervising the administrative support staff, managing departmental budget and overseeing AP/AR, acting as public relations representative for the department, managing services and professional contracts, and acting as liaison to local law enforcement agencies and county officials. Salary: $44,400.

Forensic Toxicology Laboratory Manager

The ______ State Patrol is seeking applicants for the position of Forensic Toxicology Laboratory Manager. Qualifications include a bachelor's degree in the biological or physical sciences, a minimum of three years' experience in the supervision or management of a forensic toxicology laboratory engaged in postmortem and human performance forensic toxicology, court-qualification to testify as an expert on the effects of alcohol and/or drugs, and a familiarity with current analytical standards, instrumentation, and technology. Familiarity with Drug Recognition Expert (DRE) and breath alcohol testing issues as well as experience in business operations, laboratory accreditation, and quality program development will be considered a plus.

Responsibilities include administering a program of analytical and interpretive forensic toxicology; planning, organizing, and evaluating various functions of the toxicology laboratory such as servicing law enforcement agencies, coroners, and medical examiners throughout the state; supervising and managing operations of the laboratory; testifying in judicial forums on toxicological issues; supervising staff; writing standard operating procedures; overseeing quality control programs; and preparing and maintaining laboratory accreditation. Salary: $57,708–$70,332.

Assistant, Associate, or Full Professor

______ University is seeking applicants for the position of Assistant, Associate, or Full Professor. Qualifications include a master's or doctoral degree in forensic science or a related field and a minimum of two years teaching experience.

Responsibilities include teaching courses in the Master of Forensic Sciences degree program, advising students, performing administrative tasks, and engaging in scholarly activities.

TEACHING THE FORENSIC SCIENCES

Most university teaching jobs require a graduate degree. In some settings a master's is sufficient; generally, though, most professors must have a Ph.D. In addition to teaching experience, many positions also require field experience, especially for the more practical, hands-on type of courses.

University instructors in the forensic sciences work under the same conditions as instructors in other fields.

Some university professors work in the field full-time or as part-time consultants, while also teaching part-time.

SALARIES FOR FORENSIC SCIENTISTS

What forensic scientists earn across the board is almost impossible to say. Salaries depend on job title, level of expertise—bachelor's through doctorate level, as well as number of years' experience—employer, and the region of the country.

As a general rule, federal agencies pay the most and local law enforcement agencies the least. Starting salaries could range from $25,000 per year to $35,000 per year, depending on the graduate's area of specialization and skills. Forensic experts with impressive credentials and many years of experience can command substantially more money.

The chapters ahead feature several firsthand accounts of forensic specialists working in the actual fields. Many provide salary information for their specific field. In addition, many of the sample jobs listed in this chapter and others also provide salary ranges.

TRAINING

Forensic science is a general term that encompasses a range of disciplines and levels of expertise. A forensic scientist could be trained at the bachelor's level in toxicology, DNA, or ballistics, for example. A forensic scientist could also be a Ph.D. psychologist who studies criminal behavior, profiles criminal suspects, and presents testimony in court; or a Ph.D. forensic anthropologist who specializes in reconstructing skulls to identify remains.

The type of training forensic scientists pursue depends on their area of interest and the number of years they are willing to invest. Forensic scientists who function mainly as criminalists, specializing in one or more areas of forensic evidence (DNA, handwriting analysis, and so on), may pursue a bachelor's degree or go on for a graduate degree. Forensic medicine specialties, for example, would, in most cases, require a medical degree.

Those who pursue undergraduate degrees in forensic science often use that degree as a stepping-stone to graduate work—in law, allied health and medicine, and engineering, to name a few.

It is important to note that some—even many—forensic scientists don't necessarily start their careers working in forensics. A psychologist might earn a Ph.D. in clinical psychology, not sure during his or her schooling what the ultimate job setting will be. Opportunities for consulting and other forensic work might come along gradually over time, before developing into a full-time career. The same can hold true for the accident investigator, the fire safety officer, the physical anthropologist, who more and more gets involved with forensic work and eventually replaces the original full-time career focus.

The specific training required for the different forensic specialties are covered in the chapters ahead. Included here as examples are two sample undergraduate and graduate programs for forensic science. (In Appendix D you'll find a list of colleges and universities that offer forensic science programs.)

Sample Programs

The two schools whose programs are profiled here are provided as examples; their inclusion is not meant as an endorsement, nor is the exclusion of other programs meant to indicate disapproval.

John Jay College of Criminal Justice
445 West Fifty-ninth Street
New York, NY 10019
www.jjay.cuny.edu

John Jay College offers the bachelor of arts or bachelor of science degree in fields that focus on criminal justice, fire science, and related areas of public service: Computer Information Systems, Correctional Studies, Criminal Justice, Criminal Justice Administration and Planning, Criminology, Deviant Behavior and Social Control, Fire Science, Fire Service Administration, Forensic Psychology, Forensic Science Government, Judicial Studies, Justice Studies, Legal Studies, Police Studies, Public Administration, and Security Management.

John Jay's bachelor of science in forensic science is designed "to provide training for students seeking to work in forensic science laboratories, or who are planning to pursue careers as scientists or scientist-administrators. The major draws from the biological sciences, from physics and chemistry (organic, physical, and analytical), and from the law. Students may specialize in one of two tracks: Criminalistics or Toxicology."

CRIMINALISTICS TRACK

Freshmen

Modern Biology

General Chemistry

Sophomores

Organic Chemistry

Quantitative Analysis

Forensic Science Survey of Criminalistics or Environmental Science Introduction to Environmental Science

General Physics

Juniors

Physical Chemistry II

Biochemistry

Forensic Science Laboratory (2)

Law and Evidence

Seniors

Forensic Science Laboratory Internship

Instrumental Analysis (2)

TOXICOLOGY TRACK

Freshmen

Modern Biology

General Chemistry

Sophomores

Organic Chemistry

Quantitative Analysis

Law and Evidence

General Physics

Juniors

Physical Chemistry II

Biochemistry

Instrumental Analysis (2)

Toxicology: Forensic Pharmacology

Seniors

Forensic Science Laboratory Internship

Toxicology of Environmental and Industrial Agents

Analytical Toxicology

Master's Programs

Master's programs at John Jay College of Criminal Justice include the following programs and fields:

Master of Arts in Criminal Justice

Master of Public Administration

Inspector General Program

Master of Arts in Forensic Psychology

Master of Science in Forensic Science

Master of Science in Protection Management

These master's programs complement baccalaureate degree study and may lead to doctoral study. The programs also provide for an opportunity to pursue new areas of specialization and are designed to meet the needs of pre-career, in-career, and in some cases, second-career students.

Doctoral Program in Criminal Justice

The City University of New York Ph.D. Program in Criminal Justice is located at John Jay College and is administered by the Graduate School and the University Center of The City University of New York. The program prepares students for teaching, research, and policy development careers.

Courses are taught by John Jay faculty and faculty from other senior colleges of The City University of New York. Doctoral students in criminal justice are encouraged to take some of their electives in related disciplines such as sociology, political science, philosophy, economics, and psychology.

Virginia Commonwealth University
816 West Franklin Avenue
Richmond, VA 23284
www.vcu.edu

Virginia Commonwealth University offers a Bachelor of Interdisciplinary Studies with a specialization in forensic science. "Students learn the theory and practice of forensic science, including: the nature and scope of the discipline; the application of forensic science to crime, police investigation, and the adjudication process; clinical and statistical predictions of criminal behavior, classifications of offenses and offenders, and the legal and ethical issues these engender; and the fundamental natural science and laboratory skills required for forensic work.

"The specialization in forensic science will provide students with a solid education preparing them for effective professional careers in crime laboratories, police agencies, and/or to pursue graduate studies. Students will also be prepared to pursue advanced degrees in, to name a few.... They will be exposed to principles of drug analysis, DNA analysis, trace evidence, criminalistics, and legal issues. They will be able to scientifically analyze evidence and explain its meaning in a criminal justice setting. The forensic science specialization consists of 120 credits. Students also will qualify for a minor in chemistry by completing the specialization."

FORENSIC SCIENCE CORE COURSES

Introduction to Biological Sciences I, Introduction to Biological Sciences Lab I

Introduction to Biological Sciences II, Introduction to Biological Sciences Lab II

General Chemistry I, General Chemistry Lab I

General Chemistry II, General Chemistry Lab II

Introduction to Forensic Science

Justice System Survey

General Physics

Forensic Science Specialization Requirements

Cell Biology Experimental Methods

Genetics Organic Chemistry

Organic Chemistry Lab I

Organic Chemistry II, Organic Chemistry Lab II

Quantitative Analysis, Quantitative Analysis Lab

Criminalistics and Crime Analysis, Criminalistics and Crime Analysis Lab

Forensic Criminology

Forensic Evidence and Criminal Procedure

Forensic Science Internship

General Education

Students also will select courses from the approved lists found in the VCU Undergraduate and Professional Programs Bulletin in the following general education and electives areas:

Written Communications
Mathematical and Statistical Reasoning
Precalculus Mathematics
Basic Practices of Statistics
Ethical Principles
Natural Sciences
Visual and Performing Arts
Literature
Civilization
Foreign Language
Human Behavior
Urban Environment
Justice System Survey
Medicinal Chemistry
Biochemistry
Instrumental Analysis
Clinical Immunology
Clinical Instrumentation
Criminal Law
Foundations of Criminal Justice
General Physics

Internships

Most university departments of forensic science strongly encourage students who have no previous forensic science or criminal justice experience to participate in one or more internships in a criminal justice agency or forensic science laboratory. While most of these internships are almost always unpaid, internships can provide valuable experience and a foot in the door when it comes time to land full-time employment. A list of labs and agencies where interns can be placed are provided in Appendix C.

CHAPTER 2

FORENSIC EVIDENCE

Because of the enormous range of human activity that might be involved in a crime or at a crime scene, the amount of material that could be physical evidence is almost uncountable.

Evidence may be microscopic, such as DNA or a tiny particle of skin, or it may be as large as a motor vehicle left behind at the scene. It could be as subtle as an unlocked window and whatever the implications of that are. Or it could be as obvious as a blood-covered knife lying next to a body.

Forensic evidence provides the largest arena in which forensic scientists, also known as criminalists, can show their expertise. Because of the wide range of evidence, criminalists and forensic scientists often specialize in a particular area or two. However, some specialists, especially those working in labs, must master more than one area.

But all, no matter what the specialty, must be able to examine, analyze, identify, and interpret a range of physical evidence. They must be able to apply the techniques of the physical and natural sciences while examining evidence, with the end goal to prove the existence of a crime or connect suspects to the crime. They also must often present their findings in a court of law. The information the forensic scientist collects is provided to investigators, attorneys, judges, or juries.

CRIME SCENE RECONSTRUCTION

One of the most important tasks facing the criminalist is to be able to interpret the results of findings to determine the circumstances at the time a crime occurred, or perhaps to support a statement made by a witness.

Reconstructing the events of a crime is often very difficult. Forensic scientists use scientific methods, physical evidence, and deductive and inductive reasoning to gain knowledge of the events that surround the commission of a crime.

To reconstruct a crime or crime scene requires an understanding of human behavior and the physical laws and processes involved.

Any findings must be conveyed to the other elements of the criminal justice system. This is usually done by written reports or expert testimony. The criminalist must express conclusions so that technical details are understood by the court and the jury.

SPECIALIZATIONS

A variety of criminalists and forensic scientists study the scene of the crime to gather information and evidence.

- A chip of paint from a car is found on the clothes of the victim of a hit-and-run. The paint is analyzed and the make of car is now known.
- Skin particles are found under the fingernails of an assault victim. Its DNA is analyzed and is matched to the DNA of a suspect.
- A bullet fired into a homicide victim is shown not to come from a gun a suspect owns.
- A blood spatter pattern appears confusing. What are those tiny marks along the floor, wall, and ceiling? A forensic entomologist proves how insects disturbed the crime scene.

These are just a few examples of how forensic scientists help prove how a crime did—or didn't—happen.

They study hair, fibers, blood and seminal stains, alcohol, drugs, paint, glass, botanicals, soil, flammable gases, and insulating material. They must be able to restore smears or smudged markings. They must be able to identify or compare firearms and bullets. They must be able to identify tool markings and shoeprints.

In this chapter we will examine more fully the areas of forensic photography and image enhancement, questioned documents/handwriting examination, toxicology and drug analysis, and trace evidence (hair, paint, fibers).

Forensic Photography and Image Enhancement

Forensic photographers are generally employed by police departments, coroners, sheriff's offices, and related law enforcement agencies. Their primary duty is to photograph evidence and document crime scenes, and operate the photo lab and darkroom.

Some law enforcement agencies have changed the job title from forensic photographer to titles such as *imaging specialists* or *digital image enhancement specialists* because they work with both traditional photography and digital technologies.

Digital technology originated in the 1970s and came into serious forensics use in the 1990s. It is now being used by police agencies, as well as district attorneys and defense attorneys.

Digital imaging can be used to enhance a fingerprint or videotape, an X-ray, or an audio tape. Digital imaging firms, such as Imaging Forensics (see the owner's firsthand account later in this chapter) also use digital imaging technology to create dynamic courtroom presentations.

They, similar firms, and some forensic science programs offer training in digital imaging. Many police agencies that employ forensic photographers provide on-the-job training.

Questioned Documents

Document examiners answer questions regarding authorship, authenticity, alterations, additions, and erasures to documents such as wills, contracts, anonymous notes, deeds, medical records, income tax records, time sheets, contracts, loan agreements, election petitions, checks, and other documents.

They also deal with handwriting, typewriting, the authenticity of signatures, photocopying processes, writing instruments, sequence of writing, and other elements of a document in relation to its authenticity or spuriousness.

A document examiner also may be called on to determine the significance of inks, paper, writing instruments, business machines, and other features of documents.

After forensic document examiners perform their analysis, they prepare a report of their findings. The examiner also must often go to court and testify as an expert witness.

Questioned document courses are offered as part of criminal justice, police science, or forensic science college-level programs.

Some forensic document examiners are trained on the job or have a job that sponsors their training. Trainees need a bachelor's degree. The training covers a two-year apprenticeship under the supervision of a court-qualified examiner. A trainee studies the leading texts pertaining to questioned documents, performs supervised casework, prepares court exhibits, and conducts independent research.

Document examiners are employed by large police departments as well as most state and federal law enforcement agencies.

Some of the well-known agencies include: the Federal Bureau of Investigation; the Royal Canadian Mounted Police; the United States Secret Service; the United States Immigration and Naturalization Service; the United States Postal Inspection Service; the Internal Revenue Service; Revenue Canada—Customs, Excise, and Taxation; and the United States Army Crime Laboratory.

Some examiners work privately and can be found in most major cities.

Many qualified examiners are members of the American Academy of Forensic Sciences, the American Society of Questioned Document Examiners, and are certified by the American Board of Forensic Document Examiners. The American Board of Forensic Document Examiners is the only certifying body, although there are other organizations with similar sounding names.

The board aims to safeguard the public interest by ensuring that anyone who claims to be a specialist in forensic document examination does, in fact, possess the necessary skills and qualifications.

At the time of application for certification, applicants must be engaged in the full-time practice of forensic document examination. (Exceptions are evaluated on an individual basis.)

Applicants also must take comprehensive written, practical, and oral examinations that are based on a wide range of problems frequently encountered in document examination.

For more details about qualifying for certification contact the American Board of Forensic Document Examiners (ABFDE). Their address and website are provided in Appendix A.

Toxicology and Drug Analysis

Toxicology is the study of the harmful effects of chemicals, drugs, or poisons on living systems. Toxicologists pay particular attention to the conditions under which the harmful effects occur.

Forensic toxicology refers to the interpretation of findings as they apply to the law. Findings often are used in a court of law to assist the judge or jury in making a decision.

There are three additional definitions for forensic toxicology: human-performance forensic toxicology, postmortem forensic toxicology, and forensic urine drug testing.

Human-performance forensic toxicology determines the presence or absence of ethanol and other drugs and chemicals in blood, breath, or other appropriate specimen(s) and evaluates their role in modifying human performance or behavior. This would be used, for example, to determine if someone was driving while intoxicated.

Postmortem forensic toxicology determines the presence or absence of drugs and their metabolites, chemicals such as ethanol and other volatile substances, carbon monoxide and other gases, metals, and other toxic chemicals in human fluids and tissues, and evaluates their role as a determinant or contributory factor in the cause and manner of death.

Forensic urine drug testing determines the presence or absence of drugs and their metabolites in urine to demonstrate prior use or abuse. With the sophistication of medicine and the recreational uses of drugs and alcohol, the role of toxicologists is very important. They are often asked to work with emergency room staff to determine the cause of a coma, for example. They assist law enforcement officers to determine the cause of unsafe driving. Or they assist a medical examiner to determine the cause of death. To complete their tasks, toxicologists often must work with only a small sample of blood, urine, or stomach contents. Interpretation of the results often requires the joint effort of doctors, coroners, and forensic scientists.

As with other specialties, training comes from extensive study in B.A. forensic science or criminalistics programs, B.A. chemistry programs, and to some extent, on-the-job training.

Trace and DNA Evidence

Trace evidence refers to hair, fiber, paint/polymer, and glass, and could include gunshot residue. Trace and DNA evidence experts must have a bachelor's degree in chemistry, forensic science, biology, or biochemistry. Trace evidence experts also must be familiar with the use of specialized equipment, including a variety of microscopes. They must know the proper collection (from the bodies of victims of violent crimes, from crime scenes, and from accidents), examination, and documentation procedures of trace evidence samples.

To become a Fellow of the American Board of Criminalistics (ABC) in the trace evidence specialty, it is necessary to successfully complete the Trace Evidence Specialty Examination and proficiency tests.

The Trace Evidence Specialty Examination consists of three modules: a core module all applicants must pass, and a module covering fiber/hair and paint/polymer, one of which must be successfully completed at the same time as the core module.

Information for each of the trace evidence modules is available at the ABC website, provided in Appendix A.

CREDENTIALS FOR CRIMINALISTS

The American Board of Criminalistics (www.criminalistics.com/ABC/abchome.htm) has a certification program that includes a general knowledge exam and several other specialty exams. Currently these specialty exams are offered in the fields of forensic biology, drug analysis, fire debris analysis, and trace evidence examination.

The process leading to the designation of Diplomate calls for successful completion of the general knowledge examination and continuing education. A prerequisite for this award is work experience and a bachelor's degree (in a natural or other appropriate science).

SAMPLE JOBS

The following sample job advertisements will give you an idea of the qualifications needed, the responsibilities, and the salary levels different job titles offer.

Because these listings are provided as a sample only, the employers advertising for workers are not designated. An Internet search will reveal current listings. Use keywords such as "forensics," "jobs," "careers," and "criminalistics."

Latent Fingerprint Examiner

The ______ Police Department is seeking applicants for the position of Latent Fingerprint Examiner. Qualifications include a bachelor's degree and one year of experience in fingerprint identification. Additional work experience in fingerprint identification may substitute for the required education on a year-for-year basis. An additional 5 percent pay supplement is available for IAI Latent Certification.

Responsibilities include comparing and evaluating latent fingerprints, processing physical evidence for latent fingerprints, testifying in court regarding physical and latent comparisons, and utilizing the Automated Fingerprint Identification System (AFIS). Salary: $42,272–$70,887.

Latent Print Examiner

The ______ City Police Department is seeking applicants for the position of Latent Print Examiner. Qualifications include a bachelor's degree in criminalistics, chemistry, biology, physics, or a related science from an accredited college or university; two years of experience examining and identifying latent fingerprints; and certification as a Latent Print Examiner by the Latent Print Certification Board of the International Association for Identification—or an equivalent combination of relevant education and experience in examining and identifying latent fingerprints. Salary: $38,093–$46,597.

Chemist

______ County is seeking applicants for the position of GC/MS Chemist. Qualifications include education and experience equivalent to a bachelor's degree in a job-related field of study and three years of additional experience.

Responsibilities include applying scientific principles and using special instrumentation, particularly gas chromatography-mass spectrometry, to quantitatively and qualitatively analyze materials for the presence of controlled substances, other drugs, metabolites, poisons, environmental pollutants, and other substances; testifying in legal proceedings; performing method development and analysis of non-routine or complex samples; leading the installation and training for new equipment; guiding implementation of new/revised methodology; performing more complex instrument troubleshooting and repair; and performing oversight of environmental, health, and safety issues. The chemist must meet the duties and responsibilities of a Drug Chemist II and/or Toxicology Chemist II. Successful applicant must pass a criminal background check. Salary: $35,652–$42,780.

Firearms Examiner

______ County is seeking applicants for the position of Firearms Examiner. Qualifications include education and experience equivalent to a bachelor's degree in a job-related field of study and one year of related experience. Responsibilities include conducting a variety of independent physical and microscopic analyses, classifications, and identifications on all types of tool marks, firearms, ammunition, and other types of physical evidence; interpreting analytical results and preparing written opinion reports regarding findings; and testifying in legal proceedings regarding testing methods, results, and validity of testing protocols. Salary commensurate with experience.

Forensic Scientist I

The Forensic Services Division, a division of the Department of ______ State Police, is seeking applicants to fill vacant Forensic Scientist I positions in various laboratory locations throughout the state. Qualifications include a bachelor's degree in a natural/physical science and two years of experience independently performing analytical forensic laboratory procedures in a criminal justice agency without case-by-case supervision. Responsibilities include performing complex laboratory analyses on physical evidence, devising analytical approaches to casework that may include problematic research and/or generation or modification of methods, interpreting analytical results, preparing written reports, and testifying as an expert witness in courts of law. Salary: $39,000–$57,492.

Forensic Technologist, Trace Evidence Section

The _______ Police Crime Laboratory Unit is seeking applicants for the position of Forensic Technologist, Trace Evidence Section. Qualifications include a bachelor's degree in chemistry, forensic science, biology, or biochemistry and one year of laboratory experience or relevant experience as an intern in a forensic laboratory. A master's degree in forensic science may be substituted for experience.

Responsibilities include the maintenance and calibration of equipment in the trace evidence section, including a variety of microscopes, SEM, FTIR; the proper preparation of standards, reference libraries, and samples; and the proper collection, examination, and documentation of trace evidence samples. Salary: $32,700.

Forensic Scientist DNA/Trace Evidence

The ______ County Coroner's Office is seeking applicants for the position of Forensic Scientist in the DNA/Trace Evidence Department. Qualifications include a bachelor's degree, or higher, in chemistry, biology, or forensic science. Experience working in a crime laboratory is preferred. The ideal candidate for this position will possess experience with DQAlpha/Polymarker STR, SEM/EDX, FT-IR, AA, ICP, polarized light microscopy, proper evidence collection techniques, and knowledge of crime scene evidence collection.

Responsibilities include the collection and analysis of DNA evidence and trace evidence such as hairs, fibers, paint, glass, and GSR; the collection of evidence from the bodies of victims of violent crimes; the examination of vehicles; and crime scene evidence collection.

Trace Analyst

The ______ County Police Department, Forensic Services Section, is seeking applicants for the position of Trace Analyst. Qualifications include graduation from an accredited college or university with a bachelor's degree in chemistry, biology, or a related field that includes at least twenty-four semester hours in either chemistry or biology, plus two years' experience in the scientific evaluation of physical evidence, including testifying in criminal court as an expert witness.

Responsibilities include examining and analyzing physical evidence such as fibers, paint, glass, arson, and gunshot residue. Salary: $38,872–$48,418.

Criminalist

The ______ Police Crime Laboratory Unit is seeking applicants for the position of Criminalist. Qualifications include a bachelor's degree in chemistry, forensic science, biology, or biochemistry and two years of experience in general criminalistics. A master's degree in criminalistics may be substituted for one year only of experience. Court experience is desirable. Responsibilities include routine analytical and experimental work in the crime laboratory; preparing reports and findings; participating in the search and collection of physical evidence, including crime scene processing; and testifying in court as required. Salary: $39,100.

Criminalist

The ______ County Department of the Coroner is seeking applicants for the position of Criminalist. Qualifications include a bachelor's degree from an accredited college with specialization in criminalistics, chemistry, biochemistry, or a closely related scientific field that includes completion of one full year of college-level general chemistry and completion of a college-level course in quantitative analysis. A master's degree or higher in chemistry, biochemistry, or a closely related scientific field from an accredited college is highly desirable.

Under close supervision, guidance, and direction by either a senior or supervising criminalist and while participating in on-the-job training, responsibilities will include performing physical and chemical analysis of evidentiary materials such as blood, narcotics, drugs, hairs, fibers, metals, tool marks, and bodily fluids, utilizing microscopic techniques and/or comparison macro photography, chromatography, spectrography, and/or physical, analytical, and comparison techniques; participating in the preparation of written findings and displays for court presentation; testifying in court concerning findings as established by the laboratory analysis; and examining crime scenes to collect, interpret, and preserve physical evidence for analysis and evaluation. Incumbents receive work of a progressively responsible nature and of broadening scope as capabilities develop and complete comprehension with all phases of laboratory analysis is gained. Salary: $43,713–$54,248.

Criminalist I/II

The ______ County Sheriff's Office Forensic Laboratory is seeking applicants for the position of Criminalist I/II. Qualifications include advanced knowledge of general criminalistics to contribute in the laboratory's multidisciplinary environment. The ideal candidate also will have experience in the collection, analysis, and evaluation of physiological fluids and other physical evidence gathered from crime scenes and be able to participate in the laboratory's on-call, crime scene rotation schedule. Salary: Criminalist I: $46,572–$58,224. Criminalist II: $58,032–$72,540.

Criminalist II

The County of ______ is seeking applicants for the position of Criminalist II. Qualifications include a bachelor's degree from a U.S. accredited college or university, or certified equivalency for foreign studies in chemistry, biology, or a closely related field, with completed course work consisting of at least eight semester/twelve quarter units of general chemistry and three semester/four quarter units of quantitative analysis; three years of comparable, full-time experience conducting a variety of forensic examinations including the explanation and presentation of laboratory tests in a court of law as an expert witness; and proficiency in two of the following areas: analysis of solid dose narcotics and dangerous drugs; analysis of alcohol content of blood and urine in forensic samples; analysis of blood or body fluids for genetic characterization; analysis of trace evidence; analysis of blood, urine, or other materials for drugs and poisons; processing of crime scenes for physical evidence; and firearms and tool marks examination, or three years of experience as a Criminalist I.

Employees are expected to provide their own transportation (reimbursed) for travel and pass a thorough background investigation, which includes a truth verification interview. Work schedule will include irregular hours, weekends, holidays, or evenings. There will be exposure to disease and hazardous materials in the handling and analysis of evidence.

Responsibilities include performing work involved in the collection, preservation, analysis, and interpretation of physical evidence relevant to law enforcement investigations; and providing expert witness testimony regarding the results of chemical and biological tests concerning case sample analysis. Salary: $60,070–$73,008.

Forensic DNA Analyst

A private laboratory is seeking applicants for the position of Forensic DNA Analyst. Qualifications include a bachelor's degree in biology, genetics, biochemistry, molecular biology, or forensic science. Classes in biostatistics and/or population genetics a plus. Prior experience using the Applied Biosystems 310 or 377 for analysis of the CODIS 13 core loci or for DNA sequencing is highly desirable.

Responsibilities include performing DNA testing on forensic casework samples.

Forensic DNA Analyst (Casework Manager)

The ______ Health & Social Services, Office of the Chief Medical Examiner DNA Unit, is seeking applicants for the position of Forensic DNA Analyst (Casework Manager). Qualifications include at a minimum a B.A./B.S. degree or its equivalent degree in biology, chemistry, or forensic science; successful completion of college course work covering the subject areas of biochemistry, genetics, and molecular biology; and completion of course work or training covering statistics and population genetics as it applies to forensic DNA analysis. An advanced degree and testimony experience are preferred but not required.

Responsibilities include coordinating the forensic DNA caseload for the state and processing these cases using the Promega PowerPlex 16 STR system on the ABI 310 Genetic Analyzer. Primary duties include case inventory, photo documentation, serological preliminary analysis, DNA extraction, DNA amplification, STR analysis, report writing, and courtroom testimony.

Forensic DNA Examiner/Analyst

Private laboratory is seeking applicants for the position of Forensic DNA Examiner/Analyst. Qualifications include a B.S. degree plus five years experience, or an M.S. degree plus three years experience, or a Ph.D. degree plus two years experience. Degree should be in biology, chemistry, or a forensic science–related area, and applicant must have successfully completed college course work covering the subject areas of biochemistry, genetics, and molecular biology or other subjects that provide a basic understanding of the foundation of forensic DNA analysis, as well as course work and/or training in statistics and population genetics as it applies to forensic DNA analysis. Applicants also must have a minimum of six months of forensic serology and DNA laboratory experience, including the successful analysis of a range of samples typically encountered in forensic casework prior to independent casework analysis using DNA technology.

Responsibilities include the performance of forensic serological testing, trace evidence analysis, and the isolation, amplification, and typing of DNA in forensic casework biological samples. This person is responsible for specimen processing, test performance, and reporting of test results.

Forensic Drug Analyst Associate

The ______ Department of Public Safety is seeking applicants for the position of Forensic Drug Analyst Associate. Qualifications include a bachelor's degree in a natural science, criminalistics, or a closely related field.

Responsibilities include the analysis of controlled substances and testifying in court as an expert witness. Salary: $27,044.

Forensic Chemist I (Drug Chemist)

The ______ County Police Department is seeking applicants for the position of Forensic Chemist I (Drug Chemist). Qualifications include graduation from an accredited four-year college or university with major course work in chemistry and one year or more technical experience in analytical chemistry.

Responsibilities include analyzing and identifying controlled dangerous substances, utilizing modern analytical techniques and instrumentation as necessary, preparing analytical reports, and testifying in court as an expert witness. Preference will be given to applicants who have experience in the analysis and identification of controlled dangerous substances, who have forensic chemist certification from the ______ State Department of Health and Mental Hygiene (or comparable certification from another state or the American Board of Criminalistics), and who have successfully presented and defended expert witness testimony in court. Salary: $34,395–$51,900.

Forensic Consultant—Firearms Analysis Section

The ______ City Police Department is soliciting proposals for the services of a Forensic Consultant for the Firearms Analysis Section of the Police Laboratory. The primary duties and responsibilities of the consultant will be (1) to provide comprehensive training in both firearms operability examination and in forensic microscopy; (2) to create and administer competency and proficiency tests for each discipline; (3) to create and administer a program to train examiners in moot court sessions; and (4) to process cases and conduct operability and microscopy examinations when needed.

Firearms/Tool Mark Examiner

The ______ State Police Crime Laboratory is seeking applicants for the position of Firearms/Tool mark Examiner. There is a full-time position available as well as a contractual position, which may be full- or part-time. Qualifications include experience in firearms/tool mark examination work, two of which must have been as a court-recognized expert. A college degree is not required, but preferred.

Responsibilities include analyzing and comparing firearms and tool mark evidence, preparing written reports, and testifying in court as a forensic expert. Salary: $36,765–$54,963.

Forensic Document Examiner

A government laboratory in ______ is looking for an experienced Questioned Document Analyst. The GS-1397-13 level position is for a senior examiner with considerable experience as a forensic document examiner. Board Certification by the ABFDE will be necessary for consideration at the GS-13 level. Salary: $60,818–$79,063.

The GS-1397–11/12 level position will be available if fully qualified candidates cannot be found at the senior examiner (GS-13) level. Although certification is not required at this level, significant laboratory experience as a working document examiner is necessary. This is not an entry-level position. Salary for a GS-11 is $42,673 to $55,474 per year. Salary for a GS-12 is $51,144 to $66,488 per year.

FIRSTHAND ACCOUNTS

Sandra Ramsey Lines, Forensic Document Examiner

A former government examiner, Sandra Ramsey Lines is now in private practice based in Arizona. Her clients come from all over the country.

She earned an A.A. in criminal justice from Scottsdale Community College and her B.A. in management from the University of Phoenix.

She began her career with a two-year internship with the Arizona Department of Public Safety in 1991 and has been working in the field since then.

GETTING STARTED

"In the late 70s, while I was employed as a police officer/detective with the Cleveland Police Department in Ohio, I was in charge of a complicated investigation involving fraudulent checks. The city was in 'default' at the time and did not have the money to pay the document examiner who was on contract with the city. I learned of a relatively new examiner with another county laboratory. I was so impressed with him and his work that I wanted to enter the field. Although I did not have a degree at the time, he offered to train two Cleveland police officers in a two-year program. I put through a proposal with the department, but it was not acted upon at that time. Although I loved my work as a law enforcement officer, I never lost my interest in questioned document work, so when the opportunity came along years later in Arizona, I ran with it.

"While employed as a special agent with the attorney general's office of Arizona, I was privileged to work with an assistant attorney general who (along with me) recognized the need for more qualified document examiners. Together we were able to obtain a federal grant to pay my salary while I was in training. In addition we were fortunate enough to find a wonderful mentor with the state laboratory who agreed to conduct the training. It took a few years, though, for the approval process to come together and the training to begin.

"In 1996 a different attorney general made a political decision to shut down the questioned document laboratory I had established. This laboratory was 75 percent federally funded and served the Medicaid fraud units throughout the United States. I had a choice: Should I remain as a special agent with the agency and give up four difficult years of training, research, and certification preparation, or go with another agency. I retired as an Arizona law enforcement officer and became a senior forensic document examiner with the Bureau of Alcohol, Tobacco and Firearms in Walnut Creek, California. When I married two years ago, I moved back to Arizona and started a private practice."

WHAT THE WORK IS LIKE

"A forensic document examiner conducts the examination of questioned documents. We analyze and compare questioned handwriting, handprinting, typewriting, commercial printing, photocopies, papers, inks, and other documentary evidence with known materials to establish the authenticity of the contested (or questioned) material, as well as the detection of alterations.

"The examiner helps lawyers and the court by examining and offering written opinions on a variety of disputed document problems including: wills, deeds, medical records, income tax records, time sheets, contracts, loan agreements, election petitions, checks, and anonymous letters to determine identity, source, authenticity, alterations, additions, deletions, or other germane issues. In addition, a forensic document examiner (FDE) must give expert testimony and be prepared to demonstrate/support his or her findings to a court of law or regulatory body.

"To be recognized as a candidate for certification by the American Board of Forensic Document Examiners (ABFDE), the only board recognized by the American Academy of Forensic Sciences and the American Society of Questioned Document Examiners, one must possess a minimum of a bachelor's degree and successfully complete a minimum two-year, full-time training program in a qualified laboratory or with a qualified forensic document examiner (FDE) recognized by the board.

"For me the work is never boring. Each case is unique and presents its own challenges. There is no typical case. One day you can be working on a disputed will involving the possibility of forged signatures, typewriting identification, and paper insertions. The next day it may be an anonymous note or notes involving a computer-generated document.

"When I examine questioned documents, my findings may be responsible for sending someone to prison or helping someone prove their innocence. Therefore, I keep abreast of the latest research and work in my field, generally through continuing education. I conduct independent research, publish in respected scientific journals, and remain active as a member in professional organizations.

"One downside of the FDE's work in public or private practice is dealing with the attorneys who have hired (knowingly or unknowingly) nonqualified individuals who represent themselves as FDEs. Oftentimes these nonqualified individuals received their training as graphologists (nonscientific reading of one's personality from their handwriting). Some 'FDEs' purport to be 'certified' by a board with a name similar to the American Board of Forensic Document Examiners. Their 'board' does not utilize the more stringent qualifications or testing requirements of the ABFDE. It can sometimes be difficult to explain these differences in an inoffensive manner to a lay jury.

"A qualified FDE must make every effort to be impartial and avoid mistakes. A serious error can cost you your reputation and credibility in court.

"Discovering evidence that can lead to a definitive conclusion brings me a feeling of satisfaction and a job well-done. However, all cases do not have definitive conclusions, and sometimes I have to say I don't know. I must know my limitations and be prepared to consult colleagues with more experience or expertise in certain areas.

"In private practice the FDE must invest considerable sums in obtaining the proper equipment to conduct examinations. They must establish good credentials and a reputation for honesty with their clients. My findings may not be what a client hopes for, but I must be willing to give the good with the bad."

SALARIES

"An FDE in government practice can earn $20,000 to $80,000 a year, depending on their agency and credentials. In private practice, FDEs charge anywhere from $75 an hour to $250 an hour, again depending on their location and what the market will bear or what their credentials are.

"In private practice the downside may be in getting paid by the clients. Most examiners require a retainer prior to conducting examinations. Days may go by without any work, or all of a sudden you could be inundated with cases, creating a backlog. The private examiner must be prepared for either eventuality."

ADVICE FROM SANDRA RAMSEY LINES

"It is very difficult to obtain training as an FDE from a qualified examiner or accredited laboratory. My suggestion for anyone interested in this field is to obtain a forensic science degree, then apply for any position in a government laboratory. From there you have the opportunity to meet a qualified examiner and possibly obtain training—assuming you have the aptitude and patience for this very interesting discipline."

George Reis, Forensic Digital Imaging Consultant

George Reis is the owner of Imaging Forensics, a digital imaging firm, in Fountain Valley, California. He started out as a forensic photographer and has been working in the field since 1989.

GETTING STARTED

"I have always been a photographer, with experience as a photojournalist and in advertising photography. I chose the field of forensic photography purely by accident. I owned a commercial photography business that was struggling, and I decided to find a job in photography rather than continue the struggle. I looked for jobs in the newspapers' classifieds, saw a listing for a photographer with the Newport Beach Police Department, and decided to apply. I never had an interest in this type of photography or in police work in general. I thought that if I did get the job it would only be temporary. Instead, it proved to be an incredible opportunity and resulted in my consulting/training business that has been very successful. I started my consulting business because there was a strong need for someone to help other police agencies take advantage of digital imaging technology.

"After working as a forensic photographer for a couple of years, I realized that many aspects of the job could be done better with digital imaging technology. I introduced these concepts to the agency where I was working and began sharing this with other agencies. Seeing these agencies often getting bad advice from vendors, I realized there was a need for a consulting business, which I started in 1995.

"Since starting in the field of forensic photography and identification in 1989, I have taken numerous courses offered through law enforcement and forensics-based organizations. These include classes in fingerprint identification methods, crime scene investigation, and attendance at educational conferences through the International Association for Identification (IAI), Evidence Photographers International Council (EPIC), American Academy of Forensic Science (AAFS), and others.

"I would say that six or eight of us were the early users of digital technology, and I and others developed many of the techniques used for digital image processing, including enhancement and analysis."

WHAT THE WORK IS LIKE

"Forensic digital imaging is the legal use of photographs and images for documentation or analysis of crime scenes, evidence, or accident scenes. My job is unique in that I am a business owner working directly with police agencies, investigative firms, and attorneys on casework. As a digital imaging consultant, my business works in three areas. The first is consulting: helping police and investigative agencies incorporate the use of digital imaging equipment. This includes recommending equipment, writing protocols, and configuring and installing equipment.

"Next is training: teaching forensic personnel how to use the hardware and software for digital imaging, as well as the legal requirements and digital technology theory.

"The third is enhancement and analysis services: providing these services to agencies and businesses that may not have the expertise or equipment to do it themselves. This provides me with a lot of variations in my day-to-day job.

"Sometimes I'll travel across the country to teach a workshop in digital imaging or to consult with an agency on how they can implement digital imaging. Other times I am enhancing videotapes or negatives to try to get the most information from these images.

"As an example, I was given a videotape of a burglary in which the two suspects pulled up to a closed convenience store in a commercial truck, broke the glass in the front door, entered through the broken glass, stole merchandise, and then exited with the goods. By enhancing the frames of the video that showed their truck through the store window, we were able to positively identify the unique numbering on the cab of the truck. This led to an arrest, which then led to an identification and conviction of the two suspects.

"My work varies from day to day and is almost always fun. However, as a business owner, I also have to keep track of all business paperwork and tax information and spend time on promoting the business."

THE UPSIDES AND DOWNSIDES

"The most exciting aspect of my work is seeing the excitement that others get from this. For instance, when I provide training, an officer may skip lunch to continue working on a project or want to discuss digital imaging over dinner. Another fulfilling aspect is when a DA or attorney tells me that my work made a significant difference in the case.

"The most difficult part is traveling when I don't want to."

SALARIES

"A forensic photographer earns from about 25 percent less than a police officer to about 10 percent more. This depends on the agency and whether there is a senior or supervisory position available. My income, as a business owner, is based on the amount of work I do. If I am busy (which I usually am) I make more than a forensic photographer."

ADVICE FROM GEORGE REIS

"Get experience anywhere and everywhere you can. Volunteer at your local police department. Study photography, learn software applications, and learn about signal processing (if digital imaging analysis is your interest). Join organizations such as the IAI and EPIC. Attend conferences and meetings of these organizations. Ask questions, meet people, and work hard."

CHAPTER 3

ACCIDENT AND FIRE INVESTIGATION

Forty-one thousand, four hundred seventy-one people died in motor vehicle crashes in 1998. Although this is a 7 percent decrease from 1975 (the year authorities began collecting these figures), it is still an excessively high number. The 41,471 deaths occurred in 37,081 crashes involving 56,865 motor vehicles. Forty percent of the car occupant deaths occurred in single-vehicle crashes; 60 percent in multiple-vehicle crashes.

According to the U.S. Department of Transportation, motor vehicle crashes are the leading cause of death among Americans one to thirty-four years old.

Since the mid-1970s, passenger vehicle occupant deaths have represented a growing proportion of motor vehicle deaths, while deaths in all other categories have declined. Deaths in pickups and utility vehicles have more than doubled since 1975.

Speed, the kinds of vehicles involved, the roads on which they travel, and the use of alcohol or drugs all contribute to the death toll. So do insects, such as a bee or wasp that is trapped in a car.

Progress has been made in the past two decades, and the number of fatalities related to high blood alcohol concentrations has declined. Still, alcohol-impaired driving remains a major problem.

About one-third of all motor vehicle deaths involves vehicles leaving the road and hitting trees or utility poles. Frequently, alcohol is a contributing factor in these crashes.

According to the Insurance Institute for Highway Safety, the total societal cost of crashes exceeds $150 billion annually. Criminally set fires also cost big bucks—about $2 billion in property damage annually.

Although there are many types of fires, anything from a trash basket fire to a devastating forest fire, they all fall into just two categories: accidental or criminal.

An accident happens when someone falls asleep smoking a cigarette, or oily rags left in a corner suddenly ignite. Criminal fires are fires that were set on purpose. This is called arson and is punishable by law. Fires caused by bombs, understandably, also fall under the category of criminal fires.

Of the two million fires reported each year, one in every four is estimated to be arson or arson-related. Arson is the leading cause (29 percent) of nonresidential fires and the third-highest cause (13 percent) of residential fires.

Solving arson crimes also can help shed light on other crimes because many arson fires are set to cover up crimes. In some cities 20 to 25 percent of arson cases are linked to drug activity, according to a preliminary study by the U.S. Department of Justice.

There are several different motives for arson: spite, revenge, anger, and fraud. The most common kind of arson fraud is when someone's business is going bad and they decide to "sell it back to the insurance company." They hire someone to burn it or burn it themselves, and then try to collect on their insurance.

THE ROLE OF INVESTIGATORS

When a traffic accident is believed to be the result of criminal negligence—for example, caused by a drunk driver—or when a fire's origin is of a suspicious nature, professional investigators are called in.

While the police and the office of prosecuting attorneys might have their own traffic accident investigators, criminal defendants also can hire independent investigators to help prove innocence. All traffic investigators work with the goal of uncovering the truth. How did the accident happen?

Traffic investigators examine the existing scene or study photographs and videotapes of the scene. If called in much after the fact, they try to re-create the scene, and this area of investigation is called *accident reconstruction.*

They research and study lighting conditions at the time of the accident, the weather, visibility, and any other factors that might have been at play.

A forensic entomologist might be called in as well to examine the fragmented remains of insects that have impacted and lodged on the front fascia, windshield, and radiator of automobiles. Analysis of such remains can yield evidence to the probable path of an automobile through particular areas when pinpointing the location and areas of travel.

Fire investigators check into both accidental and criminal fires. The engine company first goes out and handles the firefighting. Once the fire has been put out, the lieutenant on the scene will try to determine how the fire started. If the loss appears to be more than $5,000 or so, or there is a suspicion that the fire wasn't accidental, the fire investigator comes in to do a more in-depth check.

The fire investigator would prefer to be at the scene when the fire is still burning, if possible. A fire in progress can give a lot of information. The color of the flame or the smoke can often reveal what caused the fire. How the fire reacts to water also gives clues. If the fire doesn't go right out when soaked, if it keeps coming back, then there's a good chance fuel was used.

Fire investigators also look at what part of the building is burning to try to ascertain where the fire started. After the fire has been extinguished, burn patterns in wood or carpeting also reveal clues.

They also look at wiring, fuse boxes, and circuit breaker boxes. They interview the firefighters who arrived first on the scene and ask what they saw. Were the doors unlocked? Was anyone running away? Was there broken glass lying inside or was it blown outside by the fire?

Only about 4 percent of arsonists ever get caught and convicted. But often, an arsonist will stay near the fire to watch the firefighters at work.

Some fire departments use "fire dogs"—accelerant detection canines—to sniff out gasoline or other accelerants at a fire scene. They are also taken through the crowd to uncover the arsonist, who might still have the smell of gasoline on his or her clothes.

Both accident and arson investigators often must go to court and testify. Their expert opinions are highly regarded and can be the factor that determines innocence or guilt.

TRAINING FOR INVESTIGATORS

Courses for accident investigation and reconstruction are offered at community colleges, traffic safety institutes, and four-year colleges and universities that offer bachelor's degrees in the subject. The programs can come under a variety of names or departments: traffic safety, transportation, transportation engineering, accident investigation, and so on. A program offered by Northwestern University's Center for Public Safety is provided below.

Most fire and arson investigators first go through regular firefighter training and put in their time as a firefighter. Once they are approved by their department to become an investigator, the training is an ongoing process. They attend special classes at colleges and fire academies and also go through internships with seasoned investigators. They study fire behavior, chemistry, court procedures, and how to handle evidence.

Not all fire investigators work for fire departments, though. Some, with the appropriate training and experience, find work with insurance companies or private investigation firms.

Sample Program

Northwestern University
Center for Public Safety
405 Church Street
Evanston, IL 60204
www.northwestern.edu/nucps/index.htm

The Center for Public Safety was established at Northwestern University as the Traffic Institute in 1936. The center is a national nonprofit organization that serves public agencies responsible for law enforcement, criminal justice, public safety, traffic management, and highway transportation systems. Local, county, state, and federal government agencies, as well as agencies from foreign countries, are served through programs of specialized training, continuing education, research and development, publications, and direct assistance.

The center maintains six divisions:

Accident Investigation

Transportation Engineering

Management Training Division

Police Training Division

Research and Development

School of Police Staff and Command (SPSC)

The Accident Investigation division offers a comprehensive curriculum. In addition to providing consulting services and expert-witness testimony, the division also acts as a clearinghouse in distributing accident investigation and reconstruction information to police agencies, prosecutors, and others in the public and private sectors.

SAMPLE COURSE DESCRIPTIONS

Accident Investigation for the Industry: This course is involved with gathering accident information from people, roads, vehicles; measuring at an accident scene; photography for accident investigation; speed estimating; accident reconstruction methodology; and real-life case study review (five-day course only).

Traffic Accident Reconstruction 1 and 2: Participants must possess skills normally learned during on-scene and technical accident investigation training (Accident Investigation 1 and 2) and improved with experience. These skills include the ability to prepare after-accident situation maps and classify and interpret vehicle damage; properly interpret marks on the road; and be proficient in algebra.

These courses provide the training necessary to reconstruct accidents through lectures and course material. The courses also provide the required experience through real-world case studies that the students must analyze.

Students successfully completing the two Traffic Accident Reconstruction courses will have met the minimum training requirements recommended by the National Highway Traffic Safety Administration (NHTSA) for police reconstructionists. Course content covers vehicle dynamics, basic equations of motion, Newton's law of motion, weight shift in slowing, resultant drag factor, sum of moments and forces, computation of the location of the center of gravity, heavy truck accident reconstruction, braking capabilities, speed estimates, roll-over problems, collinear and oblique collisions, kinetic energy, vehicle collapse and direction of thrust, angle of collision and maximum engagement, marks on the road, driver strategy and tactics, case presentation, testimony, report writing, and more.

Other courses include Accident Investigation I and II, Accident Investigation Photography and Vehicle Dynamics, and various others. Visit www.northwestern.edu/nucps/index.htm for the full listing and information on its other divisions.

SALARIES

Accident investigators employed by police departments or other government agencies would be paid on the same scale as other personnel. The salary would vary depending on the region of the country and the agency's budget. Beginning investigators would start at between $25,000 and $35,000 and would move up with more experience.

Accident investigators and reconstructionists working privately most often charge by the hour—anywhere from $75 to $150 per hour.

Median annual earnings of firefighters is about $31,170 nationwide. Firefighting and prevention supervisors average about $44,830. Median annual earnings of fire inspection occupations runs about $40,040.

Firefighters who average more than a certain number of hours a week are required to be paid overtime. The hours threshold is determined by the department during the firefighter's work period, which ranges from seven to twenty-eight days. Firefighters often earn overtime for working extra shifts to maintain minimum staffing levels or for special emergencies.

Fire and arson investigators employed by insurance companies are generally paid slightly higher than those working for fire departments.

SAMPLE JOBS

As with other sample jobs listed throughout this book, these jobs are meant to be viewed as samples only, and as such hiring bodies and contact information are not provided. When you are ready to look for employment, an Internet search should provide you with numerous available positions.

Forensic Chemist I

A state police crime lab in New England is seeking applicants for the position of Forensic Chemist I. Qualifications include a bachelor's degree in forensic science, forensic chemistry, or criminalistics; or a bachelor's degree in a related field such as chemistry, biochemistry, chemical engineering, biological chemical technology, and one year of experience in forensic science laboratory work.

Preference will be given to applicants with one year forensic laboratory experience in Fire Debris Analysis/Trace Evidence Analysis. Directly related experience may be substituted for education on a year-for-year basis.

Responsibilities include the examination and analysis of physical evidence through the use of chemical, physical, serological, and instrumental techniques; detecting, identifying, and comparing accelerants, accelerant residues, paint, polymers, fibers, hair, and glass; detecting and identifying blood, body fluids, and gunshot residues;

and testifying as an expert witness in courts of law. Salary: $28,246–$38,688.

Police and Fire Criminalist III

Performs advanced analyses in connection with the identification and comparison of objects and materials in a crime laboratory, and performs related administrative and supervisory assignments. May train Criminalists I and II in advanced casework and legal aspects of evidence evaluation and may execute administrative duties over one or more laboratory sections as assigned.

Requires three years of experience at a journey level in a criminalistic laboratory and a bachelor's degree in chemistry, criminalistics, or a related field. Requires knowledge of principles, methods, materials, equipment, and current techniques of criminalistics. Also requires general competency in at least ten (10) major criminalistic areas OR a master level of competency in one major criminalistic area. The 12 criminalistic areas are: 1) analytical chemistry; 2) drug identification; 3) blood alcohol; 4) forensic blood testing; 5) hair and fiber identification; 6) arson investigation; 7) polarized microscopy; 8) firearms and tool marks identification; 9) toxicology; 10) general comparative analysis; 11) technical macrophotography and photomicrography; and 12) X-ray techniques.

Other combinations of experience and education that meet the minimum requirements may be substituted. Salary: $53,976–$76,544.

FIRSTHAND ACCOUNTS

Jack Murray, Accident Investigator

Jack Murray is an accident investigator and works in traffic accident reconstruction. He has a bachelor's degree from the University of Hartford in Connecticut and an M.B.A. from the University of Connecticut in Storrs. He's also attended more than thirty-five specialized investigative seminars throughout the United States in accident investigation and reconstruction, including accident reconstruction (Texas A&M University) and accident photography and DWI/vehicular homicide (both at the Traffic Institute of Northwestern University, Evanston, Illinois).

Jack was named one of the top five investigators in America by *PI Magazine* in 1998, and one of the top twenty-five investigators of the century by the National Association of Investigative Specialists in 1999.

He is the author of five books on the subject and has been doing investigative work in this field since 1976 and accident reconstruction work since 1984. He started specializing in criminal defense of vehicular crime in 1989.

Jack is currently president of the North Texas Private Investigators Association.

GETTING STARTED

"I went to work on Wall Street after getting my M.B.A. Though I did not really enjoy the work, I made a very substantial amount of money. But a series of heart attacks at twenty-eight years of age made me realize there were more important things in life than financial rewards.

"I had worked as an insurance fire/arson investigator while going to college and decided that the investigative field might be of interest. Originally, I worked in criminal defense, but I became very interested in accident investigation where you apply the laws of physics and mathematics to motor vehicle accidents to determine the causation and effect of vehicle dynamics.

"With already having a heavy background in criminal defense work, it was a natural progression to put the two together and work on defense of vehicular crimes, such as manslaughter, criminally negligent homicide, and so on. The more involved I became in this field, the more I realized that continuing education was an absolute must, to stay abreast of the computer and scientific applications used in the field.

"At first I worked for an investigator from the Dallas County District Attorney's office, but after a few years he moved to California and I inherited his clients. In 1976 I obtained my own license as a private investigator from the Texas Commission on Private Security.

"Almost out of necessity I began learning the techniques of forensic photography. So many times our cases were won or lost on photographs that were taken, usually by someone else, at the scene of a crime.

"I work both civil and criminal cases and the basic applications are the same in both situations. But my job is to thoroughly investigate the circumstances and causation leading up to an accident and determine if in fact there was any criminal action or whether it is just a civil situation. This is a very challenging position to be in because I seldom get a case until well after it has occurred, sometimes as much as eighteen months later, and I must work with photos, measurements, and statements taken by someone else, usually a police agency. And they are the folks you are working against."

UPSIDES AND DOWNSIDES

"Sometimes it is very frustrating because of the vast resources of the state as compared to what the average defendant has at his or her disposal. Most times people only get as much justice as they can afford. Sometimes your clients are less than the pillars of the community, but your obligation is to give them as good a defense as the cream of society gets.

"My job requires substantial interfacing with law enforcement personnel, and this can be very difficult at times. Sometimes you find yourself dealing with a Kojak, and other times it's Barney Fife.

"Unfortunately, there are times when after doing the investigation or reconstruction you just have to tell some clients you can't help them. The facts of the case are not in their favor. Clients do not like this, especially when they have paid a lot of money for your services.

"There is, however, a great deal of satisfaction when you are able to keep a person innocent of a crime from going to jail. I am extremely fortunate that because I enjoy a high profile in my chosen field, I get to work on some very big cases, but it took a long time to build this reputation and to develop the skills that go with it.

"One thing this job isn't is boring; every case has some slightly different twist to it. Every client is a separate individual with different characteristics. Every attorney is different: some are budding Clarence Darrows, others are Bugs Bunny, and whether you like it or not, the attorney usually calls the shots as to how a case is ultimately presented to a jury. He or she may or may not know how to use the information you've provided, and it is your job to tactfully explain it."

SAMPLE CASES

"In a case we had, our client left a Christmas party and made a turn the wrong way onto a one-way street. He collided head-on with another vehicle, killing the other driver. After a blood test, it was determined that our client was over the legal limit and he was charged with DWI manslaughter.

"The state's position was, 'Hey, we got a drunk and we got a dead body, so what's the question?'

"We were able to prove that drunk, sober, or whatever, the traffic signs were so confusing and so badly placed, that anybody could have made that turn and had the same accident. The result was our client was given five years probation instead of fifteen years in the penitentiary.

"In another case our client hit a parked car on the side of the road in a rainstorm, killing the driver who was sitting in the parked car.

"Our client was charged with criminally negligent homicide. Using a videotape we produced under similar conditions and still photos the police took of the deceased's vehicle, we were able to prove that the car's parking lights were not on at the time of the accident, and the overhead lighting was such, that the time it took for our driver to recognize there was a vehicle parked there, and either swerve or stop, was insufficient. This time we received a verdict of not guilty."

SALARIES

"While you won't gain instant recognition in the field, you can make a very good living after a relatively short time, if you put the effort into obtaining the training and experience it takes. Because of the need to acquire experience, investigators start at relatively low wages. While certainly not minimum wages, they are comparatively low to those experienced folks make.

"A qualified reconstructionist usually charges somewhere between $100 and $150 per hour. An experienced accident investigator usually earns somewhere between $75 and $100 dollars per hour.

"Some weeks you might work seventy hours on a case and next week only five, so cash flow is sometimes very irregular, although most experienced investigators and/or reconstructionists receive a substantial retainer up front."

ADVICE FROM JACK MURRAY

"If you are interested in this kind of work, talk to your local police department and ask if you can ride along with one of their accident investigators a few times and get a feel for what they deal with in the field.

"Also, find out who your local private sector experts are, and tag along on some field work with them to see what the mechanics involve. Find your local investigative associations—every state has at least one—and go to some of their meetings and find out which members do this kind of work. Hang around and listen. Ask questions.

"For formal education, you might consider a major in criminal justice or math or physics or engineering, depending on your own aptitudes and interests. There are a very large number of community colleges in the United States that have two-year programs in criminal justice. If you add a few extra courses in math or physics, you'll be in a position to get a good offer at graduation.

"The job requires a lot of testifying under oath in depositions and trials. Recent Supreme Court decisions (1999) have set whole new guidelines for determining who can qualify as an expert in various matters before the court. This is done separately for each and every case in which you are involved. Just because you are qualified as an expert in trial A does not mean that you will automatically be qualified in case B. A good background in mathematics, physics, or engineering is a pretty basic requirement for this type of career."

Robert Lemons, Fire Investigator

Robert Lemons is a fire investigator with a South Florida fire department. He is also a trained firefighter and paramedic and the handler of Holly, an accelerant detection canine.

GETTING STARTED

"Once I became part of the fire department, I got a broader view of what goes on in the department as a whole. And while I do like riding the rescue trucks with the sirens and the lights, the fire investigation end seemed more interesting to me. I watched the investigators come in at a fire and I asked a lot of questions. Why are you doing this? Why are you looking here? What are you looking for? I was persistent. After your supervisors get to know you and see that it's not just idle curiosity but a genuine interest in the job, they help you along."

HOLLY—THE ACCELERANT DETECTION CANINE

"I was sitting in the fire station and saw a magazine article about an accelerant detection canine. That was back in 1989 or 1990. These dogs have only been around since 1988. It was a new twist on what I was already interested in. I spoke to the chief and told him that I'd like him to send me to the Maine State Police Canine Academy, in Portland, for five weeks, with a dog, to learn how to investigate fires.

"He thought that was the funniest thing he'd ever heard! But I showed him the article, did some more research, found out the success rate when using dogs, and then I went back to my chief. He realized a dog like Holly would be a good tool. So in 1990 I started looking for a dog. Holly was donated by a local family for this job. Labradors are good for this kind of work. She was three at the time.

"I looked at several dogs before I found Holly. The dog has to have the right temperament. You want a dog who is very social, who likes to be around people. She has to be curious and have a good nose. She can't be afraid of loud noises or new environments. And she can't be afraid of going into places where the footing isn't always sturdy. Holly tromps right through. She enjoys her work.

"Holly is trained to go in after a fire and search for residue of a flammable or combustible liquid such as gasoline, diesel fuel, or lighter fluid. When she finds something, she sits and signals us. We collect the samples from where she's indicated and send them to the lab. Her success rate is very high. Even if the equipment can't pick up the scent, Holly can.

"But we don't always assume that there was arson involved just because the dog sits down and signals us. There are a lot of reasons why flammable liquids are kept in the house. People might store their charcoal lighter fluid inside or gasoline for the lawn mower. Holly can find the fuel but she doesn't know if it was there legitimately. That's where the human fire investigators have to take over.

"Holly has been trained on a food reward system. The only time she eats is when she finds something. That doesn't mean she goes without her regular meals if there are no fires to investigate. On her days off, I take a little dropper of flammable liquid the chemist has prepared and put a few drops down, in the driveway or in my house. Then I put her in a work mode and have her search for this stuff. When she finds it, she gets to eat. This goes on every single day. No little treats or in-between-meal snacks.

"There's a good reason why we use a food reward. A lot of dogs are rewarded with play time. A drug dog will find a suitcase with drugs in it and will start biting and scratching it. The handler will bring out a ball or towel and praise the dog, and then the dog will grab the towel and release the article. But in a fire setting, all that playing would disturb the evidence. We need a dog that will alert by sitting very still.

Holly's training for this work involved five steps: First, through repetition, we imprinted Holly with the odor. Just as you teach a dog to sit over and over, Holly was taught that when she smells this odor (gasoline or any other accelerant), she'll get a food reward. We start with an odor contained in a can, but so she doesn't sit down every time she sees a can, we also put cans out that are empty and odorless.

"Then we put in the alert. It's a two-step passive alert—the 'sit' and 'show me.' Holly learns that in order to get fed she must find the odor, then sit. She comes in, sniffs around the can, sits down, and then I say 'show me.' Holly will put her nose directly where she smells the odor. We teach her this because, in a fire scene, everything is all black, and we have to know exactly what piece of debris has the flammable liquid on it.

"Now we transfer this process to a larger area. Instead of containing the odor in cans, we put it on the can lids, which we spread out on the ground. She then learns to check on the floor. When she's working she makes a sound like a pig rooting around, snuffling as she sniffs the area.

"We also use four or five other odorless lids. She'll see the silver thing on the ground and will sniff until she finds the one with the odor. Then she'll sit and be fed.

"Next we take her to both hot fire scenes, where we know she will find something, and cold fire scenes, where we know she won't. We want to make sure she understands she won't always find something every time she comes to a fire scene.

"Finally, we do a blind test to make sure she really is finding the odor, that it's not just coincidence. A chemist prepares five sample cans. He numbers them from one to five and puts burnt debris in each of them. But he will put a drop of accelerant in only one of the cans, and he's the only one who knows which can it is.

"We take the lids off and let Holly sniff. The chemist checks his log to see if the can she alerted was the right one."

WHAT THE WORK IS LIKE

"You meet a lot of people and interact with different agencies, the local police, the state fire marshall, the federal people. And it's always a big pleasure working with Holly. She's a good partner. But she has her moods, just like we do. There are days you don't feel like working and the same holds true for Holly. Sometimes at fire scenes or—it will always be when it's important—at a demonstration for a fire official, Holly will just look around and say, 'Not today.' You can tell she's just going through the motions.

"The rewards of this job can be few and far between. Especially when you know how a fire started, know that it was arson, but you can't prove it in a court of law. A lot of times you learn that the insurance company had to pay the claim even though you know the owner did it. You get frustrated, but inside you know you did the best job you could do. You did your part."

CHAPTER 4

FORENSIC MEDICINE

Many of us are familiar with the practice of forensic medicine from watching TV characters portray these roles. They perform autopsies to learn how a person died. But although performing autopsies plays a large role in forensic medicine, it's not the only role.

Identifying an unknown body sometimes comes into play. The forensic pathologist might utilize medical information about illnesses or operations, for example, matching known scars from a missing person to scars evident on a "found" person.

On the team might be a forensic dentist or odontologist—forensic odontology is another term for the profession of forensic dentistry—who will use dental records to identify an unknown person.

And if a body has become little more than skeletal remains, the pathologist can call in a forensic anthropologist (see Chapter 5) or an image enhancement specialist to re-create a skull and face.

Also on some forensic medical teams are forensic nurses who work with rape and assault victims and also help in death investigations.

FORENSIC PATHOLOGY

Pathology is defined as the study of disease, or any deviation from a healthy, normal condition. Pathologists examine the body at autopsy and study tissues removed during surgery. They also analyze fluids from the body, such as blood or urine, in the clinical pathology laboratory.

Forensic pathology is a specialization of pathology that applies the principles of pathology, and of medicine in general, to the legal needs of society. In other words, forensic pathologists perform autopsies to determine what caused a person's death and how the person died. Was it a natural death, accidental, suicide, homicide, or undetermined? If the death falls into the realm of criminal, then the information that a pathologist obtain from the autopsy can be used in a court of law.

Forensic pathologists often have other job titles, such as medical examiner, coroner, or medicolegal death investigator. Forensic pathologists work mainly with violent deaths—deaths due to homicide, accident, or suicide. But they also perform autopsies in other cases, including:

- sudden death of a supposedly healthy person
- unattended death (someone who had never seen a doctor)
- death while the person is in police custody
- suspicious or unusual death
- death from medical malpractice
- death while in prison

Not all deaths must be reported to the medical examiner or coroner. The laws of each jurisdiction determine that.

The Duties of the Forensic Pathologist

The forensic pathologist's work includes visiting where the subject died and gathering information about what happened at the time and place of the subject's death. The pathologist looks at what the person had been doing at the time and assesses the overall health of the person.

During the examination of the body the forensic pathologist will look closely at the person's clothing and at the exterior of the body and then will conduct an internal exam—the autopsy—concentrating on the organs in the body. The autopsy also may include the study of tissues under a microscope or through the use of x-rays.

Because various types of evidence may be collected, the forensic pathologist works in conjunction with other forensic scientists. Fingernail clippings and scrapings, swabs containing seminal fluid, hair samples, and fibers on the clothing and body are evidence in a case and are sent to crime laboratories for examination by a criminalist.

Other specimens obtained at autopsy might be sent for toxicology study. These could be stomach contents, blood, urine, bile, liver, kidney, lungs, brain, fingernail clippings, and hair. The toxicologist examines these specimens for the presence of alcohol, drugs, poisons, or other chemicals.

If bullets, shotgun pellets, or wadding are recovered at the autopsy, these are sent to the crime laboratory for examination by a ballistics expert.

During the examination of the body, the pathologist must determine which injuries were received when the victim was alive, which changes occurred after death, such as the rate of decomposition, and which injuries were received after death.

The pathologist must interpret and document patterns of change and injury. He or she must be able to state in a report, and perhaps as an expert witness, that death occurred because of bullet wounds, stab wounds, or blunt force injuries such as those that occur when beaten or when struck by a car. He or she must also determine if the blunt force injuries resulted from an accidental fall. The pattern of injuries also must be examined to rule out or confirm suspected child abuse.

The pathologist coordinates his or her findings with other available information and tries to determine if, for example, the subject died where found, or if the body was moved. The time of death is also ascertained.

The work the forensic pathologist does must be recorded through a written report and with photographs. The forensic pathologist's findings may lead to the conviction of a suspect, or it may acquit an innocent person.

Another role of the forensic pathologist is in areas of public health and safety and injury prevention. For example, a pathologist may discover that a child's death was caused by the faulty design of a crib, toy, or article of clothing. The pathologist also might learn that a vehicle's exhaust system was faulty, or the tires were defective. This information can help prevent further similar deaths or injuries.

Clinical forensic pathologists work with victims who survived certain injuries or conditions. Since these same injuries or conditions have been witnessed before through autopsies, the forensic pathologist is able to assist medical doctors in the emergency room, examine wounds, and interpret them for the attending physician and the police.

Training for Pathologists

It's a long road of training for forensic pathologists. First and foremost a pathologist must be a medical doctor. It takes many years of education and training to become a physician: four years of undergraduate school, four years of medical school, and three to eight years of internship and residency, depending on the specialty selected. A few medical schools offer a combined undergraduate and medical school program that lasts six years instead of the customary eight.

Premedical students must complete undergraduate work in physics, biology, mathematics, English, and inorganic and organic chemistry. Students also take courses in the humanities and the social sciences.

Some students volunteer at local hospitals or clinics to gain practical experience in the health professions.

The minimum educational requirement for entry to a medical or osteopathic school is three years of college; most applicants, however, have at least a bachelor's degree, and many have advanced degrees.

There are 144 medical schools in the United States—125 teach allopathic medicine and award a Doctor of Medicine (M.D.) degree; 19 teach osteopathic medicine and award the Doctor of Osteopathic Medicine (D.O.) degree.

Acceptance to medical school is very competitive. Applicants must submit transcripts, scores from the Medical College Admission Test, and letters of recommendation. Schools also consider character, personality, leadership qualities, and participation in extracurricular activities. Most schools require an interview with members of the admissions committee.

Students spend most of the first two years of medical school in laboratories and classrooms taking courses such as anatomy, biochemistry, physiology, pharmacology, psychology, microbiology, pathology, medical ethics, and laws governing medicine. They also learn to take medical histories, examine patients, and diagnose illness.

During the last two years, students work with patients under the supervision of experienced physicians in hospitals and clinics to learn acute, chronic, preventive, and rehabilitative care. Through rotations in internal medicine, family practice, obstetrics and gynecology, pathology, pediatrics, psychiatry, and surgery, they gain experience in the diagnosis and treatment of illness.

Following medical school, almost all M.D.s enter a residency-graduate medical education in a specialty that takes the form of paid on-the-job training, usually in a hospital. Most D.O.s serve a twelve-month rotating internship after graduation before entering a residency that may last two to six years.

Physicians may benefit from residencies in managed care settings by gaining experience with this increasingly common type of medical practice.

All states, the District of Columbia, and U.S. territories license physicians. To be licensed, physicians must graduate from an accredited medical school, pass a licensing examination, and complete one to seven years of graduate medical education. Although physicians licensed in one state can usually get a license to practice in another without further examination, some states limit reciprocity. Graduates of foreign medical schools can usually qualify for licensure after passing an examination and completing a U.S. residency.

Specializations

M.D.s and D.O.s seeking board certification in a specialty may spend up to seven years—depending on the specialty—in residency training. A final examination immediately after residency, or after one or two years of practice, is also necessary for board certification by the American Board of Medical Specialists (ABMS) or the American Osteopathic Association (AOA). There are twenty-four specialty boards, ranging from allergy and immunology to pathology and urology.

For certification in a subspecialty, physicians usually need another one to two years of residency. Pathologists number only about 2.4 percent of all medical doctors, making this a wide-open field to enter.

To learn more about specific requirements, visit The American Board of Pathology website at www.abpath.org/.

The Cost of Training

A physician's training is expensive, and although education costs have increased, student financial assistance has not. Over 80 percent of medical students borrow money to cover their expenses. The high salaries doctors often command are offset the first few years in practice by the need to pay back hefty student loans.

Salaries

Physicians have among the highest earnings of any occupation. According to the American Medical Association, the average annual income for pathologists after expenses is $175,000. Income will vary widely according to number of years in practice, geographic region, hours worked, and skill, personality, and professional reputation. The sample jobs listed later in this chapter include salary ranges.

FORENSIC DENTISTRY AND ODONTOLOGY

Forensic odontology, also referred to as forensic dentistry, is part of forensic medicine and the general field of the forensic sciences.

There are four general areas for which a forensic dentist offers his or her services:

1. Identification of deceased people through dental remains.
2. Bite mark analysis; determining or ruling out possible suspects in crimes in which bite marks are left on a victim or other object.
3. Examination of oral-facial structures for determining patient/doctor disputes such as possible malpractice, or to prove or disprove insurance fraud.
4. Age estimation through dental features.

Most of a forensic dentist's workload revolves around the first item: identification of deceased people. A forensic dentist is asked to help identity unknown victims of accidents, homicides, or mass disasters such as floods, earthquakes, or airline crashes.

Identification of humans by means of teeth, dental work, and other oral characteristics has been used for centuries. Here are some fascinating examples:

- In 1066 in England, a story circulated that William the Conqueror made the official seal of England by biting into the wax. He was known to have an unusual malocclusion.
- In 1477 in France, the cadaver of Charles, Duke of Burgundy, was identified by the absence of some anterior teeth.
- In 1776 in Massachusetts, General Joseph Warren's body was dug up and identified by a piece of walrus tusk that had replaced a canine tooth.
- In 1850 in the United States, John White Webster was the first person convicted of murder based on dental evidence.
- In 1906 in England, two people were convicted of burglary using bite mark evidence. One took a bite out of a piece of cheese and left it behind.
- In 1925 in the United States, a chemist attempted to defraud his insurance company by setting fire to his lab leaving an unrecognizably charred corpse behind. His new "widow" identified it as the

chemist by his two missing teeth. But upon closer inspection it was revealed that the teeth had only recently been removed—the cavities were not fully healed. The chemist had lost his two teeth years before.

- In 1948 in England, the Gorringe case was the first murder to be solved using bite mark evidence.
- In 1967 in England, Gordon Hay was convicted of murder with crucial bite mark evidence.
- In 1976 in the United States, computers were first used for dental identification in a mass disaster: 139 victims of the Big Thompson Canyon Flood.
- In 1979 in the United States, bite mark evidence was used in convicting serial killer Ted Bundy.
- In 1979 near Chicago, American Airlines Flight 191 crashed and 274 people lost their lives. Dental identification was performed by two teams of ten dentists.
- In 1979 in Guyana, computers helped with the dental identification of 913 victims of a mass cult suicide/murder led by James Jones in the People's Temple at Jonestown.

Forensic odontological identification is based upon comparing dental records made during the victim's lifetime with data collected after death. The antemortem data are usually found in dental records, which consist of X-rays, charts, impressions, and study models of the teeth, jaws, and dentures.

A forensic dentist also may be called as an expert witness to give testimony concerning scientific investigation or to provide professional opinions about evidence introduced into a trial.

Training for Forensic Odontologists

Forensic odontologists must have special knowledge in certain areas, such as being familiar with the unique characteristics of the teeth and the resistance of teeth and tooth restorations under different kinds of environmental stresses. Forensic odontologists also should be aware of the special laws and regulations that govern professional activities. The prerequisites for this field include an educational background in dentistry—preferably a doctorale degree—in addition to a D.D.S. or D.M.D.

However, there are many others—dental hygienists and assistants, for example—who help to make up the forensic dental team. Those who work on the team and are not licensed and qualified dentists would be supervised by the team leader, a professional forensic odontologist.

A dental education provides the fundamentals required for the tasks encountered during forensic work. The skills required include the ability to recognize:

each tooth in and out of the mouth,

different tooth surfaces,

types of filling materials,

racial and sociological differences in dentition, and

a knowledge of oral pathology and closeup photography.

In addition, specialized postgraduate training in the field of forensic dentistry should be pursued. There are currently several courses offered in North America and in Europe. Many of these courses teach the fundamentals of evidence collection and handling, charting systems, and autopsy protocol.

The following dental schools offer undergraduate and postgraduate training in forensic dentistry:

Loma Linda University

University of Texas

Louisiana State University

Northwestern University

University of Louisville

New York University

University of Southern California

The Armed Forces Institute of Pathology (Washington, DC)

To practice dentistry, all dentists must be licensed. To qualify for a license in most states, a candidate must graduate from a dental school accredited by the American Dental Association's Commission on Dental Accreditation and pass written and practical examinations. Candidates may fulfill the written part of the state licensing requirements by passing the National Board Dental Examinations. Individual states or regional testing agencies give the written and/or practical examinations.

Currently, about fifteen states require dentists to obtain a specialty license before practicing as a specialist. Requirements include two to four years of postgraduate education and, in some cases, completion of a special state examination. Most state licenses permit dentists to engage in both general and specialized practice.

Dentists who want to teach or do research usually spend an additional two to five years in advanced dental training in programs operated by dental schools or hospitals. Dental schools require a minimum of two years of college-level predental education. However, most dental students have at least a bachelor's degree. Predental education includes courses in both the sciences and humanities.

All dental schools require applicants to take the Dental Admissions Test (DAT). Dental school usually takes four years. Most dental schools award the degree of Doctor of Dental Surgery (D.D.S). The rest award an equivalent degree, Doctor of Dental Medicine (D.M.D.).

To become certified by the American Board of Forensic Odontology (ABFO), a reasonable amount of hands-on experience must be documented to demonstrate qualifications. There is also a two-day written examination. Recertification occurs every five years, and active participation in forensic dentistry must be demonstrated to the ABFO through submission of cases.

Training for Dental Assistants

Most assistants are trained on-the-job, though many graduate from dental assisting programs offered by community colleges, trade schools, and technical institutes. Training programs include classroom, laboratory, and preclinical instruction in dental assisting skills and related theory. Students also gain practical experience in dental schools, clinics, or dental offices. Most programs take one year or less to complete and lead to a certificate or diploma. Two-year programs through community colleges offer an associate's degree. Certification is available through the Dental Assisting National Board but is not required for employment.

Training for Dental Hygienists

A dental hygienist must be licensed by the state in which he or she chooses to practice. To receive a license, a hygienist first must graduate from an accredited school and pass both a written and clinical exam.

Most programs lead to an associate's degree, though some offer a bachelor's. A few lead to a master's degree. The associate's degree is sufficient for practice in a dental office. A higher degree is usually required for research, teaching, or clinical practice in public or school health programs.

Forensic Odontology Work Settings

Work settings include employment at a dental school or on an individual contract basis with a law enforcement agency. For those working at a dental school, the opportunity exists to teach forensic dentistry and to conduct research projects, in addition to involvement in actual casework.

Most forensic dentists today work in private practice, however. They are usually associated with the law enforcement agencies of the county in which they live or work, and they provide forensic services on a contractual basis.

The work is sporadic and unpredictable. A forensic dental consultant never knows when he or she will be called upon to help. As a result, most have other work that provides a primary income, such as a dental practice or a teaching position.

Salaries

According to the U.S. Bureau of Labor Statistics, median annual earnings of salaried dentists is $110,160. Earnings vary according to number of years in practice, location, hours worked, and specialty. Self-employed dentists in private practice tend to earn more than salaried dentists.

Median hourly earnings of dental hygienists are about $22.00. The middle 50 percent earn between $17.28 and $29.28 an hour. The lowest 10 percent earn less than $12.37, and the highest 10 percent earn more than $38.81 an hour.

Earnings vary by geographic location, employment setting, and years of experience. Dental hygienists who work in private dental offices may be paid on an hourly, daily, salary, or commission basis.

Benefits vary substantially by practice setting and may be contingent upon full-time employment. Dental hygienists who work for school systems, public health agencies, the federal government, or state agencies usually have substantial benefits.

Median earnings of dental assistants is about $10.00 per hour. The middle 50 percent earn between $8.94 and $13.11 an hour. The lowest 10 percent earn less than $7.06, and the highest 10 percent earn more than $15.71 an hour.

Hygienists and assistants assisting on a forensics team would be paid either by the hour or as part of the contract fee-for-service arrangement.

FORENSIC NURSING

Forensic nursing is a fast growing specialty in nursing. The International Association of Forensic Nurses (IAFN) hosts a website at www.forensicnurse.org/ that provides information on this new field. Currently, IAFN is the only membership organization directly serving the educational and professional needs of forensic nurses everywhere.

The definition of forensic nursing is the application of nursing science or skills to legal proceedings. Forensic nurses are registered nurses with additional training. They work with the scientific and legal investigation and treatment of trauma and/or death of victims of abuse, violence, criminal activity, and traumatic accidents.

Forensic nurses work directly with individual patients—victims and/or perpetrators—providing care, but also taking specimens for a rape kit, for example.

They provide consultation to other nursing or medical departments and to law enforcement agencies. And, as most forensics experts do, they provide court testimony in areas dealing with trauma, evidence collection, preservation, and analysis; and/or questioned-death investigative processes.

Although forensic nursing is a fairly new subspecialty, in reality, nurses have been forensic practitioners for years.

In addition to the areas mentioned above, forensic nurses also make a significant contribution in forensic psychiatric practice and in the treatment of incarcerated patients. (See Chapter 6.)

Training for Forensic Nurses

Currently, there are not many actual bachelor's-level programs in forensic nursing in the United States, although there are a few abroad.

The best route for now is to purse a B.S.N. in nursing, then take additional course work or go on for a master's degree in forensic nursing.

In all states, nursing students must graduate from a nursing program and pass a national licensing examination to obtain a nursing license. Nurses may be licensed in more than one state, either by examination or endorsement of a license issued by another state. Licenses must be periodically renewed. Some states require continuing education for licensure renewal.

Currently, there are more than twenty-two hundred entry-level R.N. programs. There are three major educational paths to nursing:

associate degree in nursing (A.D.N.)

bachelor of science degree in nursing (B.S.N.)

nursing diploma

A.D.N. programs, offered by community and junior colleges, take about two years to complete. About half of all R.N. programs are at the A.D.N. level.

B.S.N. programs, offered by colleges and universities, take four or five years to complete. About one-fourth of all programs offer degrees at the bachelor's level.

Diploma programs, given in hospitals, last two to three years. Only a small number of programs, about 4 percent, offer diploma-level degrees. Generally, licensed graduates of any of the three program types qualify for entry-level positions as staff nurses.

There have been attempts to raise the educational requirements for an R.N. license to a bachelor's degree. These changes, should they occur, will probably be made state by state, through legislation or regulation. Changes in licensure requirements would not affect currently licensed R.N.s, who would be "grandfathered" in, no matter what their educational preparation.

Individuals considering forensic nursing should carefully consider taking the B.S.N. route, since advancement opportunities would be broader. In fact, many career paths are open only to nurses with bachelor's or advanced degrees. A bachelor's degree is usually necessary for administrative positions and is a prerequisite for admission to graduate nursing programs in forensics, research, consulting, teaching, or the different clinical specializations.

Many A.D.N. and diploma-trained nurses enter bachelor's programs to prepare for a broader scope of nursing practice. They often can find a hospital position and then take advantage of tuition reimbursement programs to work toward a B.S.N. Forensic nursing programs or courses are provided in Appendix D.

Salaries

According to the U.S. Bureau of Labor Statistics, median earnings of registered nurses are about $40,690 a year. The middle 50 percent earn between $34,430 and $49,070 a year. The lowest 10 percent earn less than $29,480, and the highest 10 percent earn more than $69,300 a year.

Median annual earnings in the industries employing the largest numbers of registered nurses are as follows:

Personnel supply services	$43,000
Hospitals	$39,900
Home health care services	$39,200
Offices and clinics of medical doctors	$36,500
Nursing and personal care facilities	$36,300

Many employers offer flexible work schedules, child care, educational benefits, and bonuses.

SAMPLE JOBS

Forensic Pathologist/Assistant Medical Examiner

Medical Examiner's Office is seeking applicants for the position of Forensic Pathologist/Assistant Medical Examiner. Qualifications include being board certified in AP/CP and board certified, or eligible, in FP. Applicant must be a team player and interested in working in a friendly and exciting environment. Interest in education is a plus.

Responsibilities include performing approximately 250 forensic and nonforensic autopsies per year, acting as assistant medical examiner, and providing education and training to students and residents in forensic pathology. Salary: $65,000–$89,000.

Forensic Pathologist

University medical branch, Department of Pathology is seeking applicants for the position of Forensic Pathologist with academic qualifications appropriate for appointment at the rank of Assistant Professor. The candidate must be board certified in forensic pathology and will serve as Deputy Medical Examiner for the county.

Responsibilities include performing approximately 700 autopsies per year, certifying an additional 300 causes of death, teaching at the Medical School in the Department of Pathology, and participating in the supervision of residents and the academic autopsy service. Interested applicants should submit a curriculum vitae, a statement of personal and academic goals, and the names of three references. Salary: $95,000–$120,000.

Deputy Medical Examiner

County Coroner's Office is seeking applicants for the position of Deputy Medical Examiner. Qualifications include a license to practice medicine in the state; certification by the American Board of Pathology in anatomic pathology and certified or board-eligible in forensic pathology at time of hire; and five years of professional physician's experience in a coroner's or medical examiner's office. Special consideration will be given for pediatric pathology experience. Salary: $94,527–$146,515.

Forensic Pathologist

County Forensic Science Center is seeking applicants for the position of Forensic Pathologist. Qualifications include graduation from an accredited school of medicine, completion of a residency in anatomic pathology, one year of experience performing medicolegal autopsies, and a valid license to practice medicine. Certification in forensic pathology by the American Board of Pathology will be required at the time of appointment, or within three years, as a condition of employment. Responsibilities include performing medicolegal autopsies, testifying in court, and taking death scene calls. This is a new appointment created due to an increased caseload of the office per year. Weekend call will be once every fifth weekend. Salary: $93,000–$100,000.

Forensic Pathologist

A private forensic consultants group is seeking applicants for the position of Forensic Pathologist. Qualifications include Board Certification in Anatomic, Clinical, and Forensic Pathology and a state license.

Responsibilities include participating in a moderately active Sheriff-Coroner autopsy service in two counties. This position will join three forensic pathologists in a private group who serve the public sector. Salary: $120,000–$150,000.

Associate Medical Examiner

Medical Examiner's Office is seeking applicants for the position of Associate Medical Examiner. Qualifications include graduation from an accredited school of medicine, completion of a residency in anatomic pathology, fellowship in forensic pathology, and a valid license to practice medicine in the state. Certification of the American Board of Pathology will be required at time of appointment and Forensic Pathology within two years of employment.

Responsibilities include performing medicolegal autopsies; completing records; testifying in court; consulting with attorneys, physicians, and investigators; attending death scene calls; and approving cremations. Salary: $70,000–$90,000.

Senior Histologist

County Medical Examiner's Office is seeking applicants for the position of Senior Histologist. Qualifications include a high school diploma or G.E.D. Must be a graduate of a National Accredited Agency of Clinical Laboratory Scientist (NAACLS) accredited Histotechnology Program/Histology certification by the American Society of Clinical Pathologists, and must have a minimum of two years of full-time work experience in a histology laboratory. Practical knowledge of operation and maintenance of microtome, automatic stainer, automatic slide, coverslipper, and tissue processor is desired, as well as knowledge of laboratory safety rules, regulations, and procedures.

Responsibilities include procuring, preparing, and staining tissue sections to assist the pathologist in making microscopic diagnoses; allocating casework to the Histology Technician of the section depending on relative abilities and experiences; monitoring analytical standards to ensure consistency and high quality are maintained at all times; maintaining safe and orderly work areas according to the Medical Examiner's policies, methods manual, safety and QA/QC procedures; participating in the training and competency testing of new analysts and interns according to sectional protocols; responding to proficiency testing requirements and following all protocols; and assisting the Laboratory Director as needed.

This person will be exposed to microbiological infections present in case samples, normal laboratory chemicals, and instruments. Some heavy lifting is required. Employment is contingent upon passing a criminal background check. Salary: $22,992–$39,000.

Forensic Dentist

Forensic dentist needed to join our team of medical experts. Must be board certified and actively practicing. We are a physician-managed professional organization whose purpose is to assist attorneys in the evaluation of potential medical malpractice, personal injury, toxic tort and product liability cases.

You will be responsible for reviewing documented material (medical records, depositions, etc.) and then rendering a nonbiased, objective opinion about the merits (or lack of merit) of the case. If supportable, you will then agree to be available for review of additional records, telephone conferences, and testimony in depositions and trial appearances until the case is concluded. The annual caseload per specialist will vary. Consultation is provided on a fixed hourly fee basis.

FIRSTHAND ACCOUNT

Patricia Speck, Forensic Nurse

Patricia Speck coordinates the forensic nursing activity for the City of Memphis, Division of Public Services and Neighborhoods,

Sexual Assault Resource Center (SARC). She earned her B.S.N. in 1982 and her M.S.N. in 1985, both from the University of Tennessee, College of Nursing, Memphis. She has been working in the field for more than a dozen years.

GETTING STARTED

"In 1983 I met Dr. David Muram, a physician who started the first child sexual abuse clinic in Memphis at the local children's hospital. I worked at the same hospital, but in a different department.

"While matriculating through graduate school, I needed a research thesis topic, and the Rape Crisis Center (RCC) was publicly controversial in the early 1980s. Swirling amid and above the controversy was a group of nurses who evaluated victims and collected evidence in a community-based clinic. Since I was looking for an independent nursing role that utilized my nurse practitioner skills, I was attracted to this position. In addition, the nursing staff was supportive, rebellious, and challenging.

"While completing my graduate thesis (1982–85) and employed full-time as a family nurse practitioner at the county health department (1984–1988), I volunteered at the center and implemented my graduate research. I was then hired as a 'nurse clinician' in 1984 to see patients on a part-time basis and to train the other staff in care of the pediatric victim (since my expertise was pediatrics).

"Following several years of volunteering and conducting research at the agency, developing policies and procedures, making recommendations to the nonnursing management, and being on-call with the pool of part-time nurses, the manager decided a nurse was needed at the agency on a full-time basis and asked me to write the job description for the nursing coordinator.

"In 1988 Dr. David Muram, the medical director of the RCC, encouraged me to take the job. I took the job but recognized the role would be solitary and without parallel. As a backup, I kept my public health position as a nurse practitioner, just in case it didn't work out. I left the public health position in 1993 because this one worked out."

WHAT THE WORK IS LIKE

"I coordinate the registered forensic nurses employed by the City of Memphis Sexual Assault Resource Center (SARC). The nurses are advanced practice R.N.s who have additional training in the identification and management of victims and offenders of IPV—Interpersonal Violence.

"I'm on-call as supervisor 24/7. Although that may seem demanding, in reality I receive few calls from the police or the newer nurses.

"In a typical day I might field a call from the police dispatch, wanting to assemble the sexual assault response team (SART) because there's been an assault reported. The SART is a response team made up of a forensic nurse, a member of the law enforcement agency, and a patient advocate, who join together to create a multidisciplinary approach to the plight of the rape victim. The R.N. is the only licensed professional in the group. The police are the investigators who must determine if a crime has been committed. The advocate is the bridge between the health care response and the criminal justice system. In my agency, we now call our advocates law enforcement liaisons.

"Law enforcement may initiate the team, but any member can initiate the response. For instance, if a victim walks into the clinic and wants to report, the team is assembled. If they do not want to report a crime, the team is not assembled because the case will not move forward in the criminal justice system and there is no need for law enforcement or advocacy. The nurse examiner will provide therapeutic care and follow-up instructions to the patient and will refer her to the appropriate mental health and medical providers.

"As part of my duties, I might talk to the patient, then talk to district attorneys about evidence and court testimony in that or other upcoming trials.

"I also hire and train new nurses and students. I deal with test results of the lab work the patients undergo. I also order supplies—medical, as well as office supplies. We use a lot of camera film to document presentations, physical and growth development, and injury, especially if the video recording equipment is not functioning properly.

"I discuss cases with the nurses; I also debrief them after dealing with an assault case. Debriefing is a process of defining an event. I debrief students and staff to prevent burnout and to help model appropriate internalization of the event.

"On any given day, I may be working on a policy or procedure, schedules, or preparing payroll. If it is a Thursday morning, I will be in staffing with the rest of the professionals. Staffing occurs weekly and provides a complete review of the cases of the previous week. In our city, it may number fifteen to forty a week.

"In the event a nurse is unable to cover a shift and I cannot find a replacement, I will take the call. Another part of my job is professional training and consultation, and I teach physicians, nurses, attorneys, and judges about the forensic nurse's role and competency. Recently, I provided education through the Department of Health for beginning nurse examiners in our state.

"I am also responsible for coordinating forensic and nursing education for Memphis Sexual Assault Resource Center (MSARC) forensic nurses, and that usually occurs during staff meetings bimonthly.

"Quality assurance is a component, and feedback is solicited not only from the students and training nurses about existing nursing practice, but from the patients as well.

"In addition, I am on citywide committees. I am the OSHA educator for the agency annually and periodically provide TB screening for the staff."

SAMPLE CASES

"A table dancer was lured to a vehicle in the parking lot of her place of employment early one morning. Three unknown males beat her with their fists and raped her. When she was released, she called law enforcement to report it. Police paged the forensic nurse, who met them at the clinic. The forensic nurse called the patient advocate. The nurse provided support and crisis intervention, physically evaluated the victim's injuries, made recommendations for referral, collected evidence (physical and verbal), and treated the victim with medications to prevent infection and pregnancy.

"The forensic nurse transferred the information to law enforcement professionals and placed the evidence into a secured location, waiting for transport by law enforcement.

"The fact that the victim was a table dancer might have adversely affected the prosecution of this case, but the photographic documentation persuaded the prosecutor to move forward. However, because there were no visible injuries to the face and head, the charges were reduced to simple assault and the offenders pleaded guilty and served no jail time.

"In another case, a grandmother was undressing her four-year-old granddaughter for a bath and discovered bruises around both nipples. She was distressed because another child in her family had died from a cancer whose first symptoms were bruising on the chest, so she took the child to the local emergency department.

"The physician in the emergency department recognized the patterned injury (bite mark) and called the police, who paged the forensic nurse to come to the hospital.

"The nurse paged the advocate and they arrived at the hospital with law enforcement. The nurse collaborated with the physician before and during the evaluation. Then the nurse provided support and crisis intervention, physically evaluated the child from head to toe, collected evidence (physical and verbal), and made recommendations for referral and follow-up to the grandmother and the physician. The evidence was transported to a secured location awaiting transport by law enforcement officials.

"This patient's grandmother called the next day to tell us that the child had disclosed who had bitten her, and the police arrested the offender.

"Another forensic nurse was called to draw the suspect's blood for DNA analysis. As it turned out, I did not have to testify because DNA evidence from the saliva left on the breast matched the DNA of the offender and the offender pleaded guilty."

UPSIDES AND DOWNSIDES

"I am an adrenaline junkie and thrive in busy environments. It is never boring, but the work sometimes can be emotionally traumatic—for instance, the discovery of a permanent, incurable, sexually transmitted disease in a child, or facilitating in the removal of a teenager from his or her home. On the other hand, the patient population is generally very needy, and interventions provide opportunities for patients to thrive in spite of their traumas.

"Another rewarding part of my job is training and empowering new nurses who are choosing to enter this field. The most challenging part of my job is maintaining an open and accepting mind about patients and providers—accepting that the patient may have seedy and secret activities and criminal motives that supersede their victim status. Also challenging is keeping an open mind with other professionals who verbalize their bias either for or against the victim. Lastly, I dislike non-nursing professionals who step into my practice without the proper education or licensure and tell me what should be done during the nursing evaluation and intervention with the patient."

SALARIES

"My salary in 2000 was $58,000 a year with benefits, up from $30,000 in 1988. Salary is dependent on the community market and the value placed on forensic nurses."

ADVICE FROM PATRICIA SPECK

"To become a forensic nurse provider, go to nursing school where there is a forensic nursing center to visit and observe. To become a leader, go to an accredited school of nursing that supports forensic nursing education at all levels—B.S.N., M.S.N., and Ph.D./D.N.S.

"For credibility in court, add nurse practitioner education and experience on the way. To create a comprehensive educational experience, get the forensic studies for credit while matriculating through family, community, maternal child, or psych/mental health nursing programs."

CHAPTER 5

FORENSIC ANTHROPOLOGY

As defined by the American Board of Forensic Anthropology, forensic anthropology is the application of the science of physical anthropology to the legal process. The identification of skeletal, badly decomposed, or otherwise unidentified human remains is important for both legal and humanitarian reasons. Forensic anthropologists apply standard scientific techniques developed in physical anthropology to identify human remains and to assist in the detection of crime.

Anthropologist Randy Skelton explains: "Methods and techniques to assess age, sex, stature, ancestry, and analyze trauma and disease are generally developed to help anthropologists understand different populations living all over the world at different times throughout history. When we take these methods and apply them to unknown modern human remains, with the aim of establishing identity or manner of death, then we are practicing the forensic application of osteology."

Forensic anthropologists frequently work in conjunction with forensic pathologists, odontologists, and homicide investigators to identify a decedent, discover evidence of foul play, and/or establish the postmortem interval. In addition to assisting in locating and recovering suspicious remains, forensic anthropologists work to suggest the age, sex, ancestry, stature, and unique features of a decedent from the skeleton.

Increasingly forensic anthropologists are being used to identify the remains of victims of homicides, mass disasters, and political atrocities.

Forensic anthropologists also deal with other issues. For example, Smithsonian Institution forensic anthropologist Douglas Ubelaker examines the problems of the homeless in contemporary society. "By looking at the pattern of trauma and disease on the skeleton we could learn a lot about his lifestyle, which in turn tells us something about the biology of the homeless."

THE BRANCHES OF ANTHROPOLOGY

There are three major subfields or branches of anthropology—cultural, archaeological, and physical. Some also include linguistics as a fourth subfield.

Cultural anthropology deals with the different and varied aspects of human society, culture, behavior, beliefs, ways of life, and so on. It can study both nontechnologic societies and technologic societies, past and present.

Archaeology is the study of past cultures, through peoples' material remains and artifacts. The lifestyles of past peoples can be studied from what they leave behind. This can range from small shards of pottery to large dwellings such as huts or houses of worship. Archaeological research covers a vast array of cultures throughout time and space—from prehistory on up to our recent past, all over the world.

Forensic anthropologists will find it useful to be familiar and comfortable with archaeological methods used in the uncovering of artifacts. Other disciplines that can overlap with archaeology include geology, geography, ecology, and history.

Physical—also known as biological—anthropology deals with the physical and biological aspects of the primate order: humans, chimps, gorillas, monkeys, and so on, both past and present.

Some of the specialized areas covered under this largest subfield of anthropology include:

- primatology—the primate biology and behavior
- osteology—the study of bones

- paleoanthropology—the study of primate evolution
- paleodemography—vital statistics of past populations
- skeletal biology
- human variation and adaptation
- genetics
- nutrition
- dental anthropology

Most forensic anthropologists are primarily trained in physical anthropology. Forensic anthropology is an "applied" area, borrowing methods and techniques developed from skeletal biology and osteology and applying them to cases of forensic importance.

Some forensic anthropologists are skilled in the art of facial reproduction. This involves the modeling of how a face may have appeared in the living subject using the only surviving evidence—a skull. Artists and sculptors also work in this area.

Other forensic anthropologists have developed skills in the determination of time elapsed since death by examining insect remains and states of body decomposition.

Forensic anthropologists, with their naturalistic approach to recovery of skeletons, examination of animal remains, and analysis of soil and vegetation patterns, can successfully recover human remains from different kinds of terrain, for example, deserts or forests.

TRAINING

There are no actual programs in forensic anthropology. Students can major in anthropology at the undergraduate level, then go on for a master's, or preferably a Ph.D., specializing in physical anthropology or anatomy.

Those who want to pursue forensic anthropology seek out a mentor, take additional courses and workshops in related forensic sciences, and participate in internships in appropriate settings, such as in a medical examiner's office.

Because most forensic anthropologists work in universities, a Ph.D. is almost always the basic requirement.

Forensic Anthropologist Dr. A. Midori Albert, who provides a first-hand account at the end of this chapter, offers the following advice:

"The best way to approach your education in forensic anthropology is to realize that, above all, you are an anthropologist first...your specialty in the applied area of forensic science is secondary. Basically, all forensic anthropologists are anthropologists, but not all anthropologists are forensic anthropologists.

"At the undergraduate level, you do not want to specialize. You will most likely be required to take classes in each of the three subfields of anthropology to ensure your breadth of training:

- cultural anthropology: behaviors, rituals, belief systems, economies, kinship, traditions, history, language, art, etc., of various societies throughout the world, past and present
- archaeology: reconstructing the lives of ancient or historic peoples from their material remains (artifacts), or studying what modern people leave behind
- physical/biological anthropology: aspects of human beings themselves—bones, diet and nutrition, growth, disease, reproduction, adaptation, human evolution; aspects of primates—behaviors, evolution, and ecology

"The above list may also include linguistics (study of language), depending on where you choose to study anthropology.

"In short, as an undergraduate student (working on your bachelor's degree), it's a good idea to familiarize yourself with many different areas of anthropology first. From a solid foundation you can then branch out and specialize. For example, you can focus on physical anthropology, where you may wish to specialize in osteology, which can later be applied to forensic settings.

"Additionally, you could benefit greatly from courses in genetics, biology, chemistry, physics, anatomy/physiology, zoology, and statistics. Many of these classes also will satisfy your basic studies or core freshman and sophomore requirements.

"To be admitted to graduate school in anthropology, you should have a bachelor's (B.A.) in anthropology, or at the very least a minor or its equivalent. By equivalent I mean at least one anthropology survey course in each of the subfields: cultural, archaeology, physical, and language and culture or linguistics (if offered). Statistics would be great, and is highly recommended. A history and theory class in anthropology would further enhance your minor, if it's not already required. Any undergraduate courses in anatomy/physiology or vertebrate anatomy also would be a tremendous benefit. I highly recommend genetics.

"Concentrate on earning a high grade point average (GPA), and strive to earn the best score you can on the Graduate Record Examination (GRE). There are prep classes, books, CD-ROMS, etc., to help you here.

"Additionally, any undergraduate research you can do is a major plus. Get to know your professors. Find out what research they're involved in and make time to volunteer. Good—and not just mediocre—recommendation letters from your professors who know you are vital.

"Develop your writing skills; a well-written, concise, informative essay goes a long way in making a good first impression in an application packet.

"In searching for an M.A. program, don't worry about going into a program where there is no forensic anthropologist on the faculty. Find an excellent osteologist or skeletal biologist with whom to study, to be your mentor. What you need at this level is a solid background in physical anthropology, and more importantly, osteology. Become proficient with statistics. Learn to identify bones, how to analyze them, what interpretations and explanations can be made from those analyses—in every context, not just the forensic context. The forensic applications can be learned later, at the Ph.D. level or even beyond. And, after a good foundation at the M.A. level, it will be all the more easy to understand the forensic applications of bone analyses.

"If you happen to be applying to a program where you can study the forensic applications of osteology at the M.A. level, then go for it. My point here is that it's not necessary; but if the opportunity is there, by all means go with it.

"In applying to graduate school, you may apply to programs offering both the M.A. and Ph.D., or to programs offering the M.A.

"Many people go to one school for their B.A., then another for their M.A. and Ph.D.; still others go to one school for the B.A., another for the M.A., and yet another for the Ph.D. The idea here is that you get different perspectives from different anthropologists on aspects of the field. In a sense, you are trying to avoid academic inbreeding and expand your way of thinking.

"On average, many people finish the M.A. in anthropology in about two to three years, sometimes more. The Ph.D. varies even more widely. It's not uncommon for it to take five to eight years, sometimes more. Also, it takes time to gain experience teaching; many graduate students in anthropology go on to become professors and community college teachers or lecturers, so teaching experience is important.

"Many graduate students become teaching assistants (T.A.s) and conduct labs or discussion sections of classes for undergraduate students.

"In summary, it may take as few as five years or up to eight or ten years to get your M.A. and Ph.D. in anthropology—if you're going to specialize in osteology or skeletal biology. You may learn the forensic applications along the way, or you may choose to learn them at the postdoctorate level (post-doc). It is important not to rush. What good are the degrees if you're not well-trained, not confident in what you know, and have no jobs to apply for? Timing is more important than time."

JOB SETTINGS

Unfortunately, forensic anthropology offers few opportunities for full-time employment. Virtually all the forensic anthropologists in the United States have Ph.D.s in anatomy or physical anthropology; with very few exceptions, they occupy academic positions in departments of anthropology or archaeology and do forensic anthropology as a sideline.

Those working outside the university environment are employed by medical examiner's offices or law-enforcement agencies, work as curators in museums, or work in local, state, or federal crime labs as a regular staff member who just happens to have expertise in forensic anthropology.

Others work for the army, which hires a few forensic anthropologists at their forensic centers in Hawaii and Washington, DC.

They also can be self-employed, offering their services nationally to federal agencies or to any local law-enforcement agency that doesn't have a nearby forensic anthropologist to rely on.

FINDING A JOB

The American Anthropological Association (AAA) operates a placement service designed to aid anthropologists in their search for jobs and to facilitate communication between job seekers and employers. At the annual meeting the placement service is open free of charge to all association members; it provides job boards that list available jobs, a message center for communication between job seekers and employers, and interview space.

Registrants for the year-round placement service receive advance copies of "position open" forms that employers file with the placement service at the annual meeting, referrals to nonacademic jobs from employers recruiting placement service candidates, and other services such as making your resume available to employers.

To obtain forms and further information about the Placement Service, contact AAA Placement Service, 4350 North Fairfax Drive, Suite 640, Arlington, VA 22203-1620.

Other outlets for job hunting are the usual networking, classified ads in local papers for law enforcement agencies, and in the Chronicle of Higher Education for academic placement.

SAMPLE JOB

Full-time Faculty Position

______ University, Department of Sociology, Anthropology, and Criminal Justice invites applications for a full-time, tenure-track faculty position at the assistant level. The position offers the opportunity to teach law and other graduate students. Requirements include: Ph.D. in anthropology or justice or law-related fields; teaching expertise in the area of legal anthropology and in one or more of the following areas—juvenile delinquency, gender, family, victimology, comparative criminal justice, violent crime and/or organized crime. Demonstrable record of research and publication in these or related fields and a commitment to teaching excellence are required.

FIRSTHAND ACCOUNT

A. Midori Albert, Forensic Anthropologist

A. Midori Albert is an assistant professor in the anthropology department at the University of North Carolina at Wilmington. In his role as forensic anthropologist, he is a consultant with the military and local law-enforcement agencies.

He earned his B.A. in psychology with a minor in anthropology in 1990 from the University of Florida in Gainesville. He earned his M.A. in anthropology from the University of Florida in 1993 and his Ph.D. in anthropology from the University of Colorado at Boulder in 1995.

He began studying forensic anthropology as a graduate student in 1991 and started working at the University of North Carolina in 1995.

Workshops in forensic sciences he has attended include the International Forensic Photography Workshop, given through the Dade County Medical Examiner Department in Miami, Florida, and the Medicolegal Death Investigators' Training Course in St. Louis, Missouri.

GETTING STARTED

"I was fascinated by the human skeleton and human variation in general, across time and space. The idea that we could learn about diet, nutrition, trauma, how a person lived and died, was amazing to me. When I discovered that one could examine unknown contemporary skeletons to assist in establishing identity and manner of death, I knew that was what I wanted to do.

"I also liked the academic environment. I enjoy discovery and learning new things. I like the detective work, the puzzle-solving aspect of the forensic sciences. To be a professor where I can teach, conduct research, and offer consultations on forensic cases is so rewarding because I get to do the many different things I like."

WHAT THE WORK IS LIKE

"Forensic anthropology is the application of methods and theories derived from the specializations of human osteology, skeletal biology within the subfield of anthropology known as physical or biological anthropology, and some archaeology, another subfield of anthropology.

"Forensic anthropologists draw on skeletal data, formulae, and gross observations to establish an identity profile—to determine sex, age, ancestry, stature—and assess pathology (trauma and/or disease), as well as determine how long a body has been dead. Essentially, forensic anthropologists assist in the identification of people from their skeletal remains and help assess the manner of death.

"My job is varied and a typical day is hard to define. The following are activities I engage in throughout the semester, and they may fall out in any given combination:

- I teach courses in general physical anthropology, human osteology, forensic anthropology, primate biology and behavior, dental anthropology, and direct independent study projects.
- I attend departmental and university committee meetings (the business end of academia).

- I work in my laboratory, collecting skeletal data, running statistical tests, and analyzing results.
- I may spend part of the day writing a journal article. Much of forensic anthropology is about research and providing the very data we all rely on when consulting on cases.
- I may be consulting on a forensic case.

"When I do consult on a forensic case, it's usually not planned. The phone rings, or there's an E-mail about a set of unknown bones. Our medical examiner in the state of North Carolina is unusual in that he seems to like working with decomposed remains. As a result, he often does his own osteological analyses—which is not common in most states. I typically consult with the military. About forty-five miles north of Wilmington is a marine base, Camp LeJeune. I also have assisted in forensic cases for the Naval Criminal Investigative Services (NCIS), whereas most forensic anthropologists work with the medical examiner.

"I also have assisted local law enforcement (sheriff's and city police) in the identification of human vs. nonhuman remains. I have searched wooded areas for human remains; and I have been present for the draining of a pond in search of human remains.

"Questions of family genealogy and the mystery of unmarked graves have brought people to my lab. I excavated a grave to help identify a family member, and I have consulted on how to find clandestine graves.

"I want to convey that it's not like we're some weird lab scientists with bubbling potions and ghosts flying around, working in a dark dingy musty basement lab (like morgues are often depicted in movies). Rather, my lab has two sunny windows and walls in a happy, soothing color. I find my workday is quite pleasant, really, aside from occasional odors.

"The other thing I've found, not through any objective scientific inquiry, is that most folks in the forensic sciences have wonderful senses of humor. I believe it's because the work can be depressing, and naturally optimistic people balance this out.

"Not all of my work directly involves dead bodies and hands-on activities. There is really a lot of variation among forensic anthropologists in terms of what constitutes our daily duties. I also contribute to the field of forensic science by conducting workshops for law enforcement personnel. Proper search and recovery methods are a must, and I find this is a major way forensic anthropologists can contribute to the entire team approach to forensic science. It truly is a multidisciplinary effort."

UPSIDES AND DOWNSIDES

"What I like most about my work is the constant challenge and change—new research topics, new students, new cases. I also like the flexibility in my schedule and the freedom to explore areas I believe need more research.

"What I like least about my work is the struggle to bring the realization and appreciation of the multidisciplinary approach to the forefront of people's minds. Sometimes I get tied down with the business end of things, leaving less time to study the bones."

SALARIES

"I earn $45,000+ a year; this is for a nine-month contract. The "+" means that it varies from year to year because I'm involved in many activities that generate additional income, for example, online courses, workshops, consulting, and so on.

"Forensic anthropologists' salaries vary, much like any other profession. Physicians, attorneys, auto mechanics, celebrities all earn different salaries. As a university professor, my salary may differ from those forensic anthropologists who work for medical examiner offices or for government agencies. What I like best about my compensation is the chunk that goes to retirement and health insurance. It's a pretty beefy package when you include those things."

ADVICE FROM A. MIDORI ALBERT

"It's my opinion that only people who want to do what they love pursue forensic anthropology or an academic career. We don't do it for the money. The rewards are many and difficult to explain to someone who just wants to make big bucks. The luxury of time to think and interact with colleagues and students and lay people is wonderful.

"If you love bones, in any context, not just the forensic, and if you truly want to satisfy your intellectual curiosity and keep your mind working in amazing ways, then this field is for you. The education and training process can be long and arduous, but if bones are what you love, then the process is just as enjoyable as the outcome.

"To get started, major in anthropology. You can explore the American Anthropological Association Guide to Departments. This is a reference book published annually, listing all the anthropology departments in the United States, the faculty, their areas of research/expertise, whether there are graduate programs, and so on.

"There are no degrees offered in forensic anthropology, though. The field of study is anthropology, the focus is the subfield of physical/biological anthropology, and the specialization may be human osteology/skeletal biology with a forensic component. The anthropology department here offers an undergraduate degree in anthropology. At the undergraduate level, the emphasis is on breadth. Exposure to cultural anthropology, archaeology, physical anthropology, human evolution, genetics, primates, adaptation and variation, osteology, history and theory, and statistics is of utmost importance.

"I do offer undergraduate research opportunities for our majors interested in various osteology projects. This is a great opportunity to gain experience (which makes graduate research easier), to get an edge in applying to graduate school (because you've been able to demonstrate your abilities and show your serious interest), and to basically have fun.

"Investigate where you want to go, and find a human osteologist or skeletal biologist active in research. This will ensure you get a strong, broad background forming a solid foundation in osteology. From there, you can specialize in the forensic aspects of human osteology.

"It's not necessary to work with a forensic anthropologist as an undergraduate or as an M.A. student. Most people begin studying forensic anthropology as graduate students or even after the Ph.D. as a post-doc because of the advanced level of statistics, anatomy, and other areas that are needed to be understood.

"There's much to know and it doesn't all happen overnight. Be patient and gather as much information and experience as you can. Intern at a medical examiner facility, if possible. Volunteer to work in osteology labs. Be willing to do volunteer work to gain hands-on experience. Attend an archaeology field school if you can to learn excavation techniques.

"The downside of this career is that there are very few jobs. When I explored this career back in 1990, my professor told me there would be no jobs. I went for it anyway, thinking that if I have a passion for what I do, then I'd be good at it. And, if I were good at it, surely I could find some way to make a living. I believe I'm extremely fortunate to be where I am today. But, it's like my Ph.D. professor said, 'The harder you work, the luckier you get.' So, it's not luck as much as it is tenacity, patience, attention to detail, thirst for knowledge, endurance, and risk-taking that make someone successful in her/his career."

CHAPTER 6

FORENSIC PSYCHOLOGY AND PSYCHIATRY

In every law-related TV program that's on the air we're likely to see psychologists and psychiatrists get up on the witness stand and offer expert testimony. They build a case for why a defendant committed a crime, and why he or she should be acquitted. Of course, the prosecution uses expert witnesses to prove the opposite, that the defendant should be found guilty as charged.

Forensic psychologists and psychiatrists have other roles as well. They are used to evaluate a criminal defendant and assess whether he or she is competent to stand trial. They also might help a judge determine if there should be a change of venue for a trial. They work with witnesses to help restore lost memories; they assist in establishing a jury favorable to whichever side has hired the specialist; and they provide behavioral profiles to help law enforcement agencies track down and arrest criminals.

Forensic specialists also help establish guidelines for fair lineups. Or they help a worker's compensation panel determine if vocational rehabilitation plans are feasible.

Broadly defined, clinical psychology is concerned with the assessment and treatment of persons with mental disorders. Clinical-forensic psychologists are clinical psychologists who specialize in the assessment and/or treatment of persons who are involved in the legal process or legal system.

Forensic psychiatry is a subspecialty of medicine. It includes practice, consultation, and research in the areas in which psychiatry is applied to legal issues.

LEGAL ISSUES

A broad range of legal issues is addressed by forensic psychology and psychiatry. In family and domestic relations laws, issues include juvenile delinquency, child custody and visitation, parental fitness, children's need of supervision, abrogation of parental rights, spouse abuse, child neglect, abandonment of children, and adoption and foster care.

In criminal law, issues include the patient's competence to stand trial, to waive legal representation, to be sentenced, to be executed, and whether or not to consider guilt by reason of mental illness or diminished responsibility and innocence by reason of mental disease or mental defect.

Civil issues include involuntary psychiatric hospitalization; rights to refuse treatment; informed consent; competence to participate in do-not-resuscitate decisions; capacity to testify; competence to become engaged, married, or divorced; contractual capacity; disability compensation; and medical malpractice confidentiality.

WORK SETTINGS

Forensic psychologists and psychiatrists may work in secure forensic units in state forensic hospitals, community mental health centers providing specialized services, court clinics, juvenile treatment centers, jails, prisons, specialized agencies, or in private practice conducting forensic evaluation and treatment relevant to legal decision-making. It is rare, though, that a psychologist or psychiatrist in private practice limits the practice to only forensic work.

They may also be involved in teaching, training, or supervision in a department of psychology, a medical school, a hospital, an interdisciplinary institute, or a clinic.

Some professionals may also be involved in conducting research and scholarship in areas such as violence risk assessment, treatment needs and response, and decision-making strategies.

Some psychologists and psychiatrists may receive more extensive training in law and earn a J.D. (Juris Doctor) or M.L.S. (Master of Legal Studies) in addition to their training and degrees in psychology or psychiatry. These professionals involve themselves in areas of law relevant to the behavioral sciences and may work in law schools as well as in other academic, medical, or other applied settings as mentioned earlier.

In addition to teaching law, they also may become involved in research or clinical practice (depending on their specialization) or legal practice as an attorney.

SAMPLE JOBS

Psychologist II (Senior Ranking)

The Forensic Psychiatry Program of a Canadian hospital is seeking a Psychologist II. Reporting to the program manager, the selected candidate will carry out advanced professional duties as assigned, including clinical assessment and treatment of patients, program evaluation, research, and teaching. He or she will work in an interdisciplinary setting, liaise with outside agencies and professionals, and work with a degree of independence within broad guidelines and in accordance with hospital and professional standards.

A doctoral degree from an accredited clinical psychology training program is preferred, with completion of a psychology internship and at least two years of experience in a forensic mental health setting. Good communication skills and the ability to work in an interdisciplinary environment are required.

Applicants should be advised that a background check (criminal record) will be conducted.

Forensic Psychologist

State prison is seeking a Forensic Psychologist to develop institutional policies and a treatment program for offenders based on psychological theory and research, within the prison service.

Typical work activities include undertaking research projects to evaluate the contribution of specific initiatives within the prison; evaluating research and statistical data; counseling offenders to manage depression, anger, anxiety, and other presenting problems; delivering special group or therapy programs such as sex offender programs and training/counseling of prison officers; and assessing 'lifers' throughout. Additional self-employment/freelance work is possible.

Must have a Ph.D. in forensic psychology. Range of typical starting salaries: $30,000–$46,000.

Inpatient Forensic Psychiatrist

Unique clinical and clinical/academic opportunities for inpatient civil and forensic psychiatrist(s) in a state-of-the-art, university-affiliated, public psychiatric hospital.

Positions are flexible, depending on applicant's interests, experience, and training. Solid diagnostic and psychopharmacologic abilities are required. Experience is desired in one or more of the following areas: SPMI, MICA/drug abuse, forensics, or geriatric psychiatry.

Positions feature: very reasonable workload, forty-hour workweek, flexible schedule, minimal to no on-call duty, paid extra-service option, treatment of challenging patients in the context of a multidisciplinary team, time to carefully diagnose/treat without the pressures of managed care, and an extremely attractive work setting working with bright, professional, pleasant, and supportive colleagues and a supportive administration.

Positions also offer: weekly faculty-led case conferences, residency/fellowship didactics, and CME (all on-site).

There is potential for: academic appointment at the university medical center, resident teaching in the Long-Term Care Program, involvement in a forensic fellowship known for training excellence, as well as research participation (schizophrenia, SPMI, psychiatric service delivery, psychopharmacology, forensics, psychophysiology).

Benefits include competitive salary, retirement program, tax deferred savings plan, four weeks' paid vacation after one year, twelve paid holidays per year, excellent medical coverage, free dental/optical coverage, on-site day care, and employee assistance program.

TRAINING FOR FORENSIC PSYCHOLOGISTS AND PSYCHIATRISTS

Forensic psychologists major in psychology or a related behavioral science during the first four years of college. They then go on for one to two years of training for a master's degree, or go straight through for a total of four to six postgraduate years to obtain a Ph.D. in psychology.

Some psychologists then go on to take postdoctoral fellowship training in forensic psychology. Some forensic psychologists do independent study and obtain on-the-job training in forensic psychology. They then apply to the American Board of Forensic Psychology for certification through examination.

Psychiatrists are medical doctors (M.D.s) who have completed twelve years of education including college, medical school, and residency training in psychiatry. Forensic psychiatrists also have additional education and experience in areas relevant for the law.

Some forensic psychiatrists take an additional one or two years of postresidency training in psychiatry and the law. Others follow some independent study and on-the-job training.

Psychiatrists who have passed a series of examinations are then certified by The American Board of Forensic Psychiatry (ABFP).

Sample Program in Forensic Psychology

What follows is meant as an example of what a typical B.A. or B.S. program at a hypothetical college in forensic psychology would encompass.

The forensic psychology major is designed for students who are interested in the relationship between psychology and the criminal justice system. The program offers training in psychological theory, research methods, and the application of psychological principles to specific areas in the legal system. The major provides an interdisciplinary background appropriate for students who intend to pursue careers in psychology, social work, law enforcement, or other criminal justice professions.

Internship Program: Students can receive practical experience in forensic psychology by enrolling in the internship program, which offers fieldwork placements in such settings as hospitals for emotionally disturbed offenders, prisons, and agencies related to the family court.

SAMPLE BACHELOR'S-LEVEL COURSES

Courses can run the gamut from introductory psychology to higher-level courses in anthropology, sociology, government, economics, and the law:

General Psychology

Abnormal Psychology

Experimental Psychology

Psychology and the Law

Principles and Methods of Statistics

Ethics and Law

The Family: Change, Challenges, and Crisis Intervention

Social Psychology

Psychology and Women

Child Psychology

Psychology of Adolescence and the Adolescent Offender

Group Dynamics

Theories of Personality

Psychology of Alcoholism
Therapeutic Intervention in Alcoholism
Introduction to Counseling Psychology
Key Concepts in Psychotherapy
Research Methods
Criminology
Juvenile Delinquency
Drug Use and Abuse in American Society
Social Psychology and the Criminal Justice System
Psychological Foundations of Police Work
Correctional Psychology
Family Conflict and the Family Court
Psychology of Criminal Behavior
Fieldwork in Forensic Psychology
Independent Study
Psychological Analysis of Criminal Behavior
Youth, the Family, and Criminal Justice
Psychology of Oppression
Culture and Personality
Systems of Law
Anthropology and the Abnormal
Techniques in Crisis Intervention
Economic Analysis of Crime
Urban Politics
Problems in Civil Rights and Civil Liberties
Violence and Social Change in America
History of Crime and Punishment in the United States
Criminal Law

Crime and Punishment in Literature

Organized Crime in America

Race and Ethnic Relations

Probation and Parole: Principles and Practices

Social Deviance

Penology

B.A./M.A. Program in Forensic Psychology: Qualified undergraduate students may enter the B.A./M.A. program and graduate with both a bachelor's and a master's degree in forensic psychology.

JOB OUTLOOK

Although the increase in managed-care systems affects the work of clinicians, those working in forensic areas are largely untouched. The fields of psychology/psychiatry and the law in general have experienced steady growth over the last twenty years. The employment outlook for forensic psychologists and psychiatrists will continue to grow.

Opportunities for people holding doctorates from leading universities in areas with an applied emphasis, such as clinical, counseling, health, and educational psychology, should have particularly good prospects.

Psychologists with extensive training in quantitative research methods and computer science may have a competitive edge over applicants without this background.

Those holding a master's degree may find jobs as psychological assistants in the community mental health field, which often requires direct supervision by a licensed psychologist. Still others may find jobs involving research and data collection and analysis in universities, government, or private companies.

Very few opportunities directly related to psychology will exist for bachelor's degree holders. Some may find jobs as assistants in rehabilitation centers or in other jobs involving data collection and analysis. Those who meet state certification requirements may become high school psychology teachers.

FORENSIC SOCIAL WORK AND MENTAL HEALTH COUNSELING

Social workers help people function the best way they can in their environment, deal with their relationships with others, and solve personal and family problems.

Social workers often see clients who face a life-threatening disease or a social problem. These problems may include inadequate housing, unemployment, lack of job skills, financial distress, serious illness or disability, substance abuse, unwanted pregnancy, or antisocial behavior. Social workers also assist families that have serious domestic conflicts, including those involving child or spousal abuse.

Through direct counseling, social workers help clients identify their concerns, consider effective solutions, and find reliable resources.

Social workers typically counsel clients and arrange for services that can help them. Often they refer clients to specialists in services such as debt counseling, childcare or elder care, public assistance, or alcohol or drug rehabilitation. Social workers then follow through with the client to ensure that services are helpful and that clients make proper use of the services offered. Social workers may review eligibility requirements, help fill out forms and applications, visit clients on a regular basis, and provide support during crises.

Social workers who work in courts and correction facilities evaluate and counsel individuals in the criminal justice system to cope better in society. Social workers enter into law-related work with expert testimony on a number of issues including adoption, child custody and visitation, and substance abuse.

Child or adult protective services social workers investigate reports of abuse and neglect and intervene if necessary. They may initiate legal action to remove children from homes and place them temporarily in an emergency shelter or with a foster family.

Criminal justice social workers make recommendations to courts, prepare presentencing assessments, and provide services to prison inmates and their families. Probation and parole officers provide similar services to individuals sentenced by a court to parole or probation.

Mental health social workers and counselors provide services for people with mental or emotional problems. Such services include individual and group therapy, outreach, crisis intervention, social rehabilitation, and training in skills of everyday living. They also may help plan for supportive services to ease patients' return to the community.

Health care social workers help patients and their families cope with chronic, acute, or terminal illnesses and handle problems that may stand in the way of recovery or rehabilitation. They may organize support groups for families of patients suffering from cancer, AIDS, Alzheimer's disease, or other illnesses. They also advise family caregivers, counsel patients, and help plan for their needs after discharge by arranging for at-home services—from meals-on-wheels to oxygen equipment. Some work on interdisciplinary teams that evaluate certain kinds of patients—geriatric or organ transplant patients, for example.

Those who go into private practice make up another category of social worker. Most private practitioners are clinical social workers who provide psychotherapy, usually paid through health insurance. Private practitioners typically have at least a master's degree and a period of supervised work experience. A network of contacts for referrals also is essential.

Although mental health counselors do not deal with the criminal justice system as much as social workers do, they still can have contact with it, especially those working in correctional facilities. In general, counselors assist people with personal, family, educational, mental health, and career decisions and problems. Their duties depend on the individuals they serve and the settings in which they work. Many perform the same or similar functions to that of the social worker.

Counselors work in schools, mental health clinics, substance abuse programs, child welfare agencies, domestic violence shelters, rehabilitation clinics, employment centers, vocational training programs, and, of course, prisons, jails, and other criminal justice-related facilities or programs.

Counselors consult and work with parents, teachers, school administrators, school psychologists, school nurses, attorneys, police, and social workers.

TRAINING FOR SOCIAL WORKERS AND COUNSELORS

A bachelor's in social work (B.S.W.) degree is the most common minimum requirement to qualify for a job as a social worker; however, majors in psychology, sociology, and related fields may be sufficient to qualify for some entry-level jobs, especially in small community agencies.

Although a bachelor's degree is required for entry into the field, an advanced degree has become the standard for many positions. A master's in social work (M.S.W.) is necessary for positions in health and mental health settings and typically is required for certification for clinical work.

Jobs in public agencies also may require an advanced degree, such as a master's in social service policy or administration. Supervisory, administrative, and staff training positions usually require at least an advanced degree. College and university teaching positions and most research appointments normally require a doctorate in social work (D.S.W. or Ph.D.).

As of 1999, the Council on Social Work Education accredited more than 400 B.S.W. programs and 125 M.S.W. programs. The Group for Advancement of Doctoral Education in Social Work listed 63 doctoral programs for Ph.D.s in social work or D.S.W.s (Doctor of Social Work). B.S.W. programs prepare graduates for direct service positions such as caseworker or group worker. They include courses in social work practice, social welfare policies, human behavior and the social environment, social research methods, social work values and ethics, dealing with a culturally diverse clientele, promotion of social and economic justice, and populations-at-risk. Accredited B.S.W. programs require at least four hundred hours of supervised field experience.

Master's degree programs prepare graduates for work in their chosen field of concentration and continue to develop their skills to perform clinical assessments, to manage large caseloads, and to explore new ways of drawing upon social services to meet the needs of clients.

Master's programs last two years and include nine hundred hours of supervised field instruction or internship. A part-time program may take four years. Entry into a master's program does not require a bachelor's in social work, but courses in psychology, biology, sociology, economics, political science, history, social anthropology, urban studies, and social work are recommended. In addition, a second language can be very helpful.

Most master's programs offer advanced standing for those with a bachelor's degree from an accredited social work program.

Formal education is necessary to gain employment as a counselor. About six out of ten counselors have a master's degree; fields of study include college student affairs, elementary or secondary school counseling, education, gerontological counseling, marriage and family counseling, substance abuse counseling, rehabilitation counseling, agency or community counseling, clinical mental health counseling, counseling psychology, career counseling, and related fields.

Graduate-level counselor education programs in colleges and universities usually are in departments of education or psychology. Courses are grouped into eight core areas: human growth and development, social and cultural foundations, helping relationships, group work, career and lifestyle development, appraisal, research and program evaluation, and professional orientation.

In an accredited program, forty-eight to sixty semester hours of graduate study, including a period of supervised clinical experience in counseling, are required for a master's degree.

In 1999, 133 institutions offered programs in counselor education, including career, community, gerontological, mental health, school, student affairs, and marriage and family counseling that were accredited by the Council for Accreditation of Counseling and Related Educational Programs (CACREP). Another organization, the Council on Rehabilitation Education (CORE), accredits graduate programs in rehabilitation counseling. Accredited master's degree programs include a minimum of two years of full-time study, including six hundred hours of supervised clinical internship experience.

In 1999, forty-five states and the District of Columbia had some form of counselor credentialing, licensure, certification, or registry legislation governing practice outside schools. Requirements vary from state to state. In some states credentialing is mandatory; in others, it is voluntary.

Clinical mental health counselors usually have a master's degree in mental health counseling, another area of counseling, or in psychology or social work. Voluntary certification is available through the National Board for Certified Counselors, Inc. Generally, to receive certification as a clinical mental health counselor, a counselor must have a master's degree in counseling, two years of post-master's experience, a period of supervised clinical experience, a taped sample of clinical work, and a passing grade on a written examination.

PSYCHIATRIC TECHNICIANS

Psychiatric technicians provide nursing and other basic care to mentally ill, emotionally disturbed, or mentally retarded patients. They also work in a forensic capacity with prisoners. (See the first-hand account at the end of this chapter.)

Psychiatric technicians participate in rehabilitation and treatment programs, help with personal hygiene, and administer oral medications and hypodermic injections following a physician's prescriptions and hospital procedures. They monitor a patient's physical and emotional well-being and report to medical staff.

Most psychiatric technicians are trained through postsecondary vocational training programs.

SALARIES

Salaries for forensic psychologists and psychiatrists vary according to the setting and nature of the work. In academic settings, the salary for a beginning assistant professor might be in the $35,000–$40,000 range. Salaries in medical school settings are typically higher, as they are established in comparison with medical professionals.

The American Medical Association provides these average annual salary figures in the different medical specialties. Note that psychiatrists, in spite of their lucrative hourly rates, fall toward the end of the list:

Radiology	$260,000
Anesthesiology	$220,000
Surgery	$217,000
Obstetrics/Gynecology	$200,000
Emergency Medicine	$195,000
Pathology	$175,000
General Internal Medicine	$147,000
General/Family Practice	$132,000
Psychiatry	$130,000
Pediatrics	$120,000

Psychiatry professors in medical school settings earn some of their salary by obtaining grants or contracts or through clinical services income.

Even in university and other interdisciplinary settings, however, there is also growing pressure on psychologists to generate sources of salary support.

There are striking differences among the different types of correctional settings. Beginning salaries for psychologists in the federal prison system can be more than $40,000 a year. Salaries are often lower in state correctional facilities or local jails. Some correctional facilities might pay different rates depending on whether the job candidate holds a master's degree or a doctorate.

Currently, a starting salary for a doctoral-level psychologist in a hospital or community clinic setting ranges between $35,000 and $40,000.

Psychologists also are able to establish a part-time practice or consulting business in addition to working with an organization. Part-time private practice allows a psychologist or psychiatrist to earn income at an hourly rate consistent with what others charge in the field and geographic area. Rates can vary a great deal—anywhere between $75 and $250 an hour—depending upon the setting and the geographic location.

Forensic psychologists do not usually provide professional services to parties involved in legal proceedings on a contingency fee basis. Hourly rates or a flat fee is offered for expert testimony and other related services. Some forensic psychologists and psychiatrists, especially those who derive most of their income from forensic work, offer occasional pro bono or reduced rate services.

The average annual salary for psychologists in the federal government was $66,800 early last year. The federal government offers psychologists with a master's degree and one year of experience a starting salary of approximately $31,200. Psychologists with a doctorate and one year of internship could start at $37,800. Some individuals with experience could start at $45,200.

According to the U.S. Bureau of Labor Statistics, median annual earnings of social workers were $30,590. The middle 50 percent earned between $24,160 and $39,240. The lowest 10 percent earned less than $19,250, and the top 10 percent earned more than $49,080.

Median annual earnings in the industries employing the largest numbers of medical social workers were:

Home health care services	$35,000
Offices and clinics of medical doctors	$33,700
Offices of other health care practitioners	$32,900
State government, except education and hospitals	$31,800
Hospitals	$31,500

Median annual earnings in the industries employing the largest numbers of nonmedical social workers were:

Federal government	$45,300
Elementary and secondary schools	$34,100
Local government, except education and hospitals	$32,100
Hospitals	$31,300
State government, except education and hospitals	$30,800

Self-employed counselors who have well-established practices, as well as counselors employed in group practices, usually have the highest earnings, as do some counselors working for private firms, such as insurance companies and private rehabilitation companies.

FIRSTHAND ACCOUNTS

William Foote, Forensic Psychologist

William Foote began his work in this field in 1973 when he was employed by the New Mexico State Penitentiary as a psychological counselor. He received his B.A., his master's, and his doctorate, all in psychology, from the University of New Mexico.

He is currently self-employed in his own private practice and has been in private practice for twenty years.

GETTING STARTED

"My interest in forensic psychology started when I worked at the New Mexico State Penitentiary as a counselor. In that position I conducted a number of psychological evaluations and did some psychotherapy with inmates in the prison. I was intrigued by the relatively normal presentation of individuals who had committed very serious crimes. This led me to begin research in that area.

"I had an internship at a maximum security hospital in California in 1976–77 and conducted my doctoral research there. My doctoral research focused on people known as 'psychopaths.' These are individuals who seem relatively normal but have no sense of connection with other people and often commit heinous crimes.

"Subsequently, I began my private practice, which consists of conducting evaluations in both civil and criminal cases. I also qualified as a diplomate by the American Board of Forensic Psychology in 1984. A diplomate is a board certification that recognizes that I am a specialist functioning at a high level of competence in the area of forensic psychology. It is earned by experience and passing a work sample review examination and a difficult oral examination."

WHAT THE WORK IS LIKE

"Forensic psychology is a broad area, generally involving the use of information from a field of psychology in a legal setting. In my own case, forensic psychology refers to the use of clinical psychology in legal matters.

"On the criminal side, I conduct evaluations with individuals who have committed a range of crimes. Some of these evaluations are designed to determine whether the person has enough awareness of what is going on to participate in his or her criminal defense. These are called 'competency to stand trial' evaluations.

"Also, I conduct evaluations to determine whether the person was suffering from such a severe mental disease or disorder at the time he or she committed a crime, that the law does not hold him or her criminally responsible. These are called 'insanity' evaluations. In addition, I conduct evaluations to determine the best course of treatment or incarceration for an individual at the time of sentencing.

"I have also worked on a number of death penalty cases in which I had an opportunity to present information to the jury that would cause them to make the penalty more or less severe for the individual. That is, to deliver the death penalty or to choose a less severe alternative such as life in prison."

SAMPLE CASES

"I can recall one case in which a girl falsely accused her grandfather of sexually molesting her. My testimony was critical in a not-guilty verdict for him. There are several other cases where an appropriate outcome occurred in the absence of a legal mechanism to get the case there. For example, in one case a woman who was quite insane at the time she committed a dual murder was going to face a trial where she would have very likely been convicted and gone to jail. Through discussions with the defense counsel, the prosecutor, and the judge, we were able to arrange for her to be committed to the state hospital. That was eight years ago, and I recently learned that she had completed her treatment and had just graduated from college.

"Forensic psychological evaluations are complex and take many hours to complete. First, I review records. In criminal cases, these may be police reports, crime scene photos, laboratory results, and witness statements. I also may review school, medical, and psychiatric records of the defendant. Then, I administer a battery of tests to the person. These include personality tests and intelligence measures. I also give some tests to make sure the person is not trying to appear more sick or well than he or she really is. Then, I will talk with the person for two to twelve hours. This allows me to gather a history and learn about the person's problems and strengths. I usually put all of this together in the form of a written report.

"In civil cases, I do a great deal of work in employment discrimination cases, including sexual harassment and cases involving the

Americans with Disabilities Act. These are very interesting because they involve the interaction between an individual and his or her job. The evaluation process is similar, although in civil cases the records may differ from those reviewed in a criminal case. In civil cases, depositions (sworn testimony taken by a court reporter) are very common. In discrimination cases, employment and Equal Employment Opportunity Commission records also may be important."

THE UPSIDES AND DOWNSIDES

"I enjoy my work because I have an opportunity to work with a broad range of individuals. At one end of the spectrum, I work with people who are the very least capable of functioning in our society and must spend most of their lives in prison. At the other end of the spectrum, I work with individuals who have had bad things happen to them, such as automobile accidents. These individuals are often quite normal, but are reacting to extreme circumstances in their lives with their own extreme emotional reactions. It is really nice to have an opportunity to help these people receive proper treatment and to help the judge or jury to understand what has happened to them.

"What I like most about my job is the variety and interest involved in the number of people with whom I am working. What I like least is the tension and stress associated with testifying in court. In this situation there is at least one person in the room who wants to make you look foolish. Preparing sufficiently to withstand cross-examination and to present sometimes complex information to a judge and jury is often difficult. Keeping one's wits and focus during cross-examination is also sometimes hard."

SALARIES

"Salaries for forensic work tend to be about 15 to 20 percent above what is charged by psychotherapists in the community. Most forensic psychologists charge by the hour. A beginning forensic psychologist can expect to earn $40,000 to $60,000 a year, if employed by a state agency. Private forensic practice tends to pay somewhat more."

ADVICE FROM WILLIAM FOOTE

"Forensic psychologists must have sufficient training in the law to understand legal terms, the legal system, and the language of legal codes and court decisions. Bridging the gap between legal standards and clinical results is the core of the job.

"Another critical part of forensic psychology is translating information from this very specialized field into language that a judge or a jury can understand. This is hard to do at times because our concepts are relatively esoteric and the judges or juries to whom we must communicate this information are relatively unsophisticated. In many ways it is like a teaching job in which educating a group of people is your primary task.

"The forensic psychologist, no matter who hires him or her, is in the court to provide unbiased information to the court. There are pressures from those who hire you to come up with results that support their case. This is a pressure that most experts are aware of and for which they attempt to compensate. However, pressures arise from other sources in ways you might not anticipate. For example, sometimes when dealing with someone who has had bad things happen to him or her, you have to guard against becoming overly sympathetic or gullible.

"The other side of that coin is the temptation to become angry with individuals who have injured or killed helpless people or children. It is only by stepping back and attempting to maintain a neutral perspective that you are able to provide the judge or jury with information that is truly helpful, as opposed to voicing just another biased view.

"Ultimately, forensic psychologists are scientific experts and have to make sure that the quality of their work meets scientific standards. Proper administration of tests, proper interview techniques, and systematic use of documentary sources such as school and medical records are parts of this task.

"Anyone wanting to be a forensic psychologist should begin by obtaining solid training as a clinical psychologist. This means graduating with a bachelor's degree in psychology, followed by a master's and doctor of philosophy degree in clinical psychology.

"Training in psychological testing and interviewing is critical. Many pursue training as a clinical psychologist, then obtain training by way of internship or a postdoctoral fellowship at a penal or clinic setting.

"A number of graduate schools now offer forensic psychology graduate programs. For those wishing to be more fully trained in the law, several universities offer joint degree programs in which you may obtain both a Ph.D. and a law degree at about the same time. If I had it to do over again, I would probably follow that course.

"Forensic psychology is a fascinating and challenging field. It requires the very best of the psychologist's work, both in conducting high-quality evaluations and consultations and in imparting accurate information to the judge and jury. The temperament required of a forensic psychologist is somewhat different than that of most psychologists who do psychotherapy. Forensic psychologists have to be able to think critically, to organize their thinking systematically, and to talk about what they know in terms that anyone can understand.

"It is work that sometimes involves big stakes. Large amounts of money, years in prison, or even a person's life depends upon how well the forensic psychologist does his or her work.

"It is also work that makes a difference. To make the legal system more fair and better informed makes ours a better society."

Jan Bailey, Psychiatric Technician

Jan Bailey is a licensed psychiatric technician in the forensic unit of Metropolitan State Hospital in Norwalk, California. She was trained through a three-year college program and has been working in the field since 1984.

GETTING STARTED

"I have always been interested in what makes people tick. Believing there is some good in everybody, I enjoy helping others.

"I was working as a nurse's aide through a registry service at a private medical hospital. When the hospital ended up short on their psychiatric unit, the director of nurses asked for a volunteer from the registry. No one wanted to go; you could see the fear on their faces. I am only five feet tall and it took a while for the director of nurses to see me waving my hand in the air. Truly she didn't see me until I hollered, 'I will! I'll go to the psych unit.'

"Everyone else breathed a sigh of relief that they didn't have to go, and I got my first introduction to working with psychiatric patients. I loved it from the get-go and decided to enroll in a psychiatric tech program to get my state license.

"It was a three-year college program, including prerequisites for the California Psychiatric Technician program. I passed the state board examination, and my license was then issued under the California Board of Vocational Nurses and Psychiatric Technicians.

"Licensure requires thirty continuing education units every two years before you can be granted a renewal. You must take upgrade classes yearly to retain employment at Metropolitan State Hospital, where I work. Also, you must pass special forensic training classes to work inside the forensic compound within the hospital grounds.

"I had always wanted to work for the state at Metropolitan State Hospital because the benefits were very good. The state had a hiring freeze on at that time, so I worked at a private hospital. But I watched the want ads more or less as a hobby. One day I noticed an ad for Metropolitan and I drove immediately to Norwalk and filled out an application. I was hired on the spot and began employment two weeks later.

"Through the years, I have worked in the chronic schizophrenic units and have loved it. But as time went on, I began to take interest in people right there inside the forensic unit who needed understanding professionals to help them. Society tends to look down upon these people.

"I had heard that the forensic units were the wave of the future, and that although these units were more dangerous when there was an altercation, the patients didn't seem to 'go off' as often as did the schizophrenics.

"I began to see forensics as a way to branch out my services as a psych tech. I began volunteering to float to the forensic units whenever they found themselves short of help. Finally I made my decision to go over to the other side of the fence."

WHAT THE WORK IS LIKE

"I work with prisoner patients who are transferred to Metropolitan State Hospital from other hospitals while waiting for their day in court. Many of my patients are supposed to be schizophrenic, and they are there waiting to become competent to stand trial. Indeed, some really are, but most are suspected of malingering or lying so they can serve their sentences in the relative comfort of our ward milieu, rather than await trial inside a jail. The longest we can hold them before trial is three years, and most hope to languish three years with us and then have their charges dropped and be returned to society.

"We don't necessarily have to cure their mental situation, but rather make them understand the charges against them and the workings of the judicial system as it applies to their individual cases.

"The forensics compound within the state hospital is a highly secure area with guard gates on all sides and a high fence topped with razor wire around the perimeter. There also are mounted video cams on all sides. Actually, with all the hospital police surveillance and the sophisticated alarm system within the compound, it's a much safer place to work—which allows me time to concentrate on helping the forensic patients, rather than worrying so much about my own safety.

"Forensics is interesting because inside the compound the prisoners and 'dangerous' criminals become just as normal and human as you and I. They need someone to help them bridge the gap between institutionalization and the outside world. Sometimes they committed their crimes when they were young, or when they were under the influence of drugs. Sometimes they were in the throes of full-blown schizophrenia, and simply needed to be put on medication. It's amazing how normal these people are when they are not committing crimes. They are someone's father, brother, sister, son, daughter, or friend.

"My job is like being a mother to forty-eight men, most of whom are in their mid-thirties and early forties, with a range of from eighteen years of age to the early seventies. Actually, the job feels like being at home with my 'second' family, only I have forty-eight kids, some of whom are older than I. But all of them treat me respectfully and as someone they know and trust.

"The job is definitely interesting. I work the 3:00 to 11:00 shift. The pace is quite busy up until about 8:00 P.M., and then it slows down for an hour of charting.

"When I first arrive, I get my assignment from the shift lead. Jobs are rotated so I usually have a job assignment different from what I did the day before. Typically, I spend the first hour making sure the guys shower and handing out clean clothing to them. Their clothing consists of old and new army issue khaki shirts and pants. The army is no longer wearing khakis; they wear all camouflage these days. So our fellas are uniformed. There is a reason for this. Since most of them are neither schizophrenic nor retarded, they look just like the staff. Often the only distinction is that they wear uniforms—and have committed a crime.

"After that it's patio break so they can get some fresh air. Then it's time for dinner and day hall leisure skills, such as keeping abreast of the evening news.

"What follows next is medication. If I am assigned to meds, I will do that job and that job only for a period of two weeks, then the assignment is rotated to someone else who will be med nurse for a two-week rotation.

"After meds, we hand out 'specials' or food items the patients have bought with their own money, which is handled through their trust office account. Each patient receives $12.50 per month, plus whatever their families have sent them to put on their books.

"The tragic thing about these patients is by the time they come to us, many of their family members have given up on them, and $12.50 is all the money they get. If they smoke, that money won't last long, and by the end of the month they are all trying to borrow from the patients more fortunate than they are.

"After specials and evening snacks, usually milk and some kind of goody provided by the state, the patients settle down to watch movies rented through a contract with a local video store. The state gives some money on an account, and the staff goes to the video store and selects a current movie. We do that until the money runs out. When that happens, staff will usually bring in movies from home for the patients to watch.

"I work forty hours per week. Having been there fifteen years, I have been able to get Fridays and Saturdays off. These patients are prisoners and we never close, so someone has to be there for each of the three shifts, twenty-four hours a day, seven days a week.

"The patients go to bed at ten on weekdays. Then it's time to do rounds and wrap up any loose ends I didn't get finished during the shift."

THE UPSIDES AND DOWNSIDES

"What I like most about my work is that I know I have worked hard to qualify for this position as guardian, mentor, sometimes hard-nosed director, and friend to people in trouble who seriously need someone to listen to them and offer educated help. Not everyone can do my job. It is specialized and professional. It pays far above normal salary, offers great benefits and vacation packages, and I take pride in being part of the state system as a licensed psychiatric technician.

"The swing shift gives me something to do in the evening when I would just be sitting at home bored anyway. And I have every day off until around 2:00 in the afternoon, when I must get ready for work. I can shop, clean, garden, jog, whatever, and then go into work just when the day begins to drag.

"What I like least about my job is that sometimes it can be very dangerous. Patients can become volatile and 'go off,' which they do from time to time.

"The state provides mandatory annual Management of Assaultive Behavior (MAB) classes to train the staff how to work together to control assaultive patients through parry and evade tactics, rather than relying on strength alone.

"These guys are all potential con artists, and we also take mandatory classes each year that warn us of the possible cons they may attempt.

"We all work together as a team. From time to time a staff member gets seriously hurt and we all think, 'it could have been me.' The plus side is I have been doing this for fifteen years and have never been hurt."

SALARIES

"Salaries are above normal and average out around $30,000 a year, and that's take home pay. There is always opportunity for overtime, and we get eleven paid holidays per year and compensatory time off over and above our vacation time. Vacation time varies but ends up being thirteen hours per month at the top of the scale.

"Usually a person who has been there as long as I have will have accumulated one month of paid vacation per year. Overtime can be taken in time or cash, your choice. We have a great retirement system, and health benefits including medical, dental, and vision. We also have a strong union that acts as an advocate when we need it."

Advice from Jan Bailey

"If there is no psych tech program in your local college or institution, I suggest you go through the R.N. program. They do the same things as psych techs except they do more paperwork. I personally would rather be a psych tech because we do more work involving the psychiatric end of nursing, and that's what interests me more than the medical aspect of my job.

"You can work as a certified nurse's aide while going through the program to familiarize yourself with the medical/psych field and hospital settings. That way it won't seem so overwhelming to you when you set foot in the forensics department of nursing.

"If you enjoy helping people, are flexible in your thinking, work well under pressure and as a team member, this is the career for you."

APPENDIX A

PROFESSIONAL ASSOCIATIONS

LAW

American Bar Association
www.abanet.org/

EVIDENCE

American Academy of Forensic Sciences and the Forensic Sciences Foundations, Inc.
P.O. Box 669
Colorado Springs, CO 80901-0669
www.aafs.org/

The American Academy of Forensic Sciences is a professional society dedicated to the application of science to the law. Membership includes physicians, criminalists, toxicologists, attorneys, dentists, physical anthropologists, document examiners, engineers, psychiatrists, educators, and others who practice and perform research in the many diverse fields relating to forensic science.

American Academy of Psychiatry and the Law (AAPL)
One Regency Drive
P.O. Box 30
Bloomfield, CT 06002
www.emory.edu/AAPL

American Board of Criminalistics (ABC)
www.criminalistics.com/ABC/

Awards diplomate status to eligible criminalists.

American Board of Forensic Document Examiners (ABFDE)
7887 San Felipe, Suite # 122
Houston, TX 77063
www.asqde.org/abfde.htm

American Board of Forensic Document Examiners is the North American board for certifying qualified examiners in forensic handwriting comparison and all other facets of forensic document examination.

American Board of Forensic Entomology
web.missouri.edu/cafnr/entomology/index.html

American Board of Forensic Toxicology (ABFT)
P.O. Box 669
Colorado Springs, CO 80901-0669
www.abft.org/

The American Board of Forensic Toxicology provides a certification program in forensic toxicology.

American Society of Crime Laboratory Directors (ASCLD)
www.ascld.org/

American Society of Questioned Document Examiners (ASQDE)
P.O. Box 382684
Germantown, TN 38183-2684
www.asqde.org/asinfo.htm

The purposes of the society are to foster education, sponsor scientific research, establish standards, exchange experience, provide instruction in the field of questioned document examination, and promote justice in matters that involve questions about documents.

Association for Crime Scene Reconstruction
www.acsr.com/

The Association for Crime Scene Reconstruction is an organization that strives to understand the complete crime scene and the necessity of reconstructing that scene to better assess the elements of the crime and to recognize and preserve evidence.

Canadian Society of Forensic Science
La Société Canadienne des Sciences Judiciaires
2660 Southvale Crescent, Suite 215
Ottawa, Ontario
Canada K1B 4W5
www.csfs.ca/

The Canadian Society of Forensic Science is a professional organization incorporated to maintain professional standards and to promote the study and enhance the stature of forensic science. It is organized into sections such as anthropology, medical, odontology, biology, chemistry, documents, engineering, and toxicology.

Forensic-Entomology
forensic-entomology.com

Concerns insects in legal investigations.

International Association of Forensic Toxicologists (TIAFT)
Laboratoire National de Sante, Divisione de Toxicologie
Centre Universitaire
162A, Avenue de la Faiencerie,
L-1511 Luxembourg
www.tiaft.org/

Members are actively engaged in analytical toxicology or allied areas. The aims of this association are to promote cooperation and coordination of efforts among members and to encourage research in forensic toxicology. The members come from the police force, medical examiners and coroners' laboratories, horseracing and sports doping laboratories, hospitals, departments of legal medicine, pharmacology, pharmacy, and toxicology.

International Association for Identification (IAI)
2535 Pilot Knob Road, Suite 117
Mendota Heights, MN 55120-1120
www.theiai.org/

The International Association for Identification strives to be the primary professional association for those engaged in forensic identification, investigation, and scientific examination of physical evidence.

International Association of Investigative Locksmiths, Inc. (IAIL)
P.O. Box 144
Mt. Airy, MD 21771
www.iail.org/

Includes locksmiths, insurance investigators, and law enforcement officers involved in forensic examination of locks and locking mechanisms.

The International Forensic Image Enhancement Society (IFIES)
http://ourworld.compuserve.com/homepages/Forensic_Expert/internat.htm

The International Forensic Image Enhancement Society was started to facilitate the exchange of information between law enforcement agencies, laboratories, and private consultants who utilize forensic digital image enhancement processes. Members are dedicated to all aspects of forensic imaging, including, but not limited to fingerprint identification, handwriting analysis, video, and facial reconstruction.

International Society for Forensic Genetics
www.usc.es/~isfh/

The International Society for Forensic Genetics is an organization responsible for the promotion of scientific knowledge in the field of genetic markers analyzed with forensic purposes.

Society of Forensic Toxicologists
P.O. Box 5543
Mesa, AZ 85211-5543
www.soft-tox.org/

The Society of Forensic Toxicologists is an organization composed of practicing forensic toxicologists and those interested in the discipline for the purpose of promoting and developing forensic toxicology.

ACCIDENT AND FIRE INVESTIGATION/RECONSTRUCTION

Aircraft Rescue & Fire Fighting Working Group (ARFFWG)
www.arffwg.org/

The Aircraft Rescue & Fire Fighting Working Group is a nonprofit international organization dedicated to the sharing of Aircraft Rescue & Fire Fighting (ARFF) information between airport firefighters, municipal fire departments, and all others concerned with aircraft fire fighting. It has more than one thousand active members in thirty-two countries.

Department of Transportation (U.S.)
www.dot.gov/

Federal Highway Administration (FHWA)
www.fhwa.dot.gov/

Fire Department Safety Officers Association (FDSOA)
www.fdsoa.org

FDSOA was established in 1989. Its mission is to promote safety standards and practices in the fire, rescue, and emergency services community.

Insurance Institute for Highway Safety
www.highwaysafety.org/

International Association of Arson Investigators (IAAI)
12770 Boenker Road
St. Louis, MO 63044
www.fire-investigators.org/

International Association of Fire Fighters
1750 New York Avenue NW
Washington, DC 20006
www.iaff.org/

International Society of Fire Service Instructors
P.O. Box 2320
Stafford VA, 22555-2320
www.isfsi.org/

National Association of Professional Accident Reconstruction Specialists, Inc. (NAPARS)
P.O. Box 65
Brandywine, MD 20613-0065
www.napars.org

NAPARS is open to all people who are interested in the fields of traffic accident reconstruction and highway transportation safety. Present membership exceeds thirteen hundred and includes police officers, engineers, consultants, and government safety personnel.

National Fire Academy
Degrees at a Distance Program
16825 South Seton Avenue
Emmitsburg, MD 21727
www.usfa.fema.gov/nfa/index.htm

Contact the National Fire Academy for information about firefighter professional qualifications and a list of colleges and universities offering two- or four-year degree programs in fire science or fire prevention.

National Fire Protection Association
1 Batterymarch Park
P.O. Box 9101
Quincy, MA 02269-9101
www.nfpa.org/

National Highway Traffic Safety Admininstration (NHTSA)
www.nhtsa.dot.gov/

National Safety Council
www.nsc.org/

National Transportation Safety Board (NTSB)
www.ntsb.gov/

Transport Canada (Canada)
www.tc.gc.ca/

United States Fire Administration
16825 South Seton Avenue
Emmitsburg, MD 21727

University of Michigan Traffic Research Institute
www.umtri.umich.edu

MEDICINE

American Association of Colleges of Nursing
1 Dupont Circle NW, Suite 530
Washington, DC 20036
www.aacn.nche.edu

Contact them for a list of B.S.N. and graduate programs.

American Association of Colleges of Osteopathic Medicine
5550 Friendship Boulevard, Suite 310
Chevy Chase, MD 20815-7321
www.aacom.org

American Board of Independent Medical Examiners
111 Lions Drive, Suite 216
Barrington, IL 60010
www.abime.org/default.asp

American Board of Medical Specialties (ABMS)
1007 Church Street, Suite 404
Evanston, IL 60201-5913
www.abms.org/

American Board of Medicolegal Death Investigators (ABMDI)
www.slu.edu/organizations/abmdi

The American Board of Medicolegal Death Investigators is an independent professional certification board that has recently been established to promote the highest standards of practice for medicolegal death investigators.

American Board of Pathology
P.O. Box 25915
Tampa, FL 33622-5915
www.abpath.org/

American Dental Assistants Association
203 North LaSalle, Suite 1320
Chicago, IL 60601-1225

American Dental Hygienists' Association
444 North Michigan Avenue, Suite 3400
Chicago, IL 60611

American Medical Association (AMA)
Department of Communications and Public Relations
515 North State Street
Chicago, IL 60610
www.ama-assn.org

American Nurses Association
600 Maryland Avenue SW
Washington, DC 20024-2571
www.nursingworld.org

American Osteopathic Association
Department of Public Relations
142 East Ontario Street
Chicago, IL 60611
www.aoa-net.org

American Society of Clinical Pathologists
2100 West Harrison Street
Chicago, IL 60612
www.ascp.org/

American Society of Forensic Odontology
American Board of Forensic Odontology
c/o The Forensic Sciences Foundation, Inc.
P.O. Box 669
Colorado Springs, CO 80901-0669
www.asfo.org/

American Society of Investigative Pathology
9650 Rockville Pike
Bethesda, MD 20814-3993
asip.uthscsa.edu/

Association of American Medical Colleges
Section for Student Services
2450 N Street NW
Washington, DC 20037-1131
www.aamc.org

Commission on Dental Accreditation
American Dental Association
211 East Chicago Avenue, Suite 1814
Chicago, IL 60611

Association for professionals involved with forensic odontology/ dentistry and certifying board.

Dental Assisting National Board, Inc.
216 East Ontario Streeet
Chicago, IL 60611

International Association for Forensic Nursing (IAFN)
IAFN Home Office
East Holly Avenue, Box 56
Pitman, NJ 08071-0056
www.forensicnurse.org/

The International Association of Forensic Nursing is an international professional organization of registered nurses formed exclusively to develop, promote, and disseminate information about the science of forensic nursing.

National Association of Medical Examiners (NAME)
1402 South Grand Boulevard
St. Louis, MO 63104
www.thename.org

The National Association of Medical Examiners is the national professional organization of physician medical examiners, medical death investigators, and death investigation system administrators who perform the official duties of the medicolegal investigation of deaths of public interest in the United States.

National League for Nursing
61 Broadway
New York, NY 10006
www.nln.org

ANTHROPOLOGY AND ARCHAEOLOGY

American Anthropological Association
4350 North Fairfax Drive, Suite 640
Arlington, VA 22203-1620
www.ameranthassn.org/

American Board of Forensic Anthropology (ABFA)
www.csuchico.edu/anth/ABFA/

The American Board of Forensic Anthropology provides a program of certification in forensic anthropology.

Archaeological Institute of America
Box 1901-Kenmore Station
Boston, MA 02215
www.archaeological.org/

Association for Feminist Anthropology Online
4350 North Fairfax Drive, Suite 640
Arlington, VA 22203-1620
www.qal.berkeley.edu/~afaweb

Association for Political and Legal Anthropology
4350 North Fairfax Drive, Suite 640
Arlington, VA 22203-1620
www.aaanet.org/apla/index.htm

National Association for the Practice of Anthropology (NAPA)
American Anthropological Association
4350 North Fairfax Drive, Suite 640
Arlington, VA 22203
www.aaanet.org/napa

National Association of Student Anthropologists (NASA)
American Anthropological Association
4350 North Fairfax Drive, Suite 640
Arlington, VA 22203
www.aaanet.org/nasa/index.htm

Society for American Archaeology
900 Second Street NE #12
Washington, DC 20002-3557
www.saa.org/

Society for Applied Anthropology (SfAA)
P.O. Box 24083
Oklahoma City, OK 73124

PSYCHOLOGY/PSYCHIATRY

Academy of Behavioral Profiling
1961 Main Street, PMB 237
Watsonville, CA 95076-3027
www.profiling.org/

The Academy of Behavioral Profiling is a professional association dedicated to the application of evidence-based criminal profiling techniques within investigative and legal venues.

American Academy of Forensic Psychology (AAFP) and The American Board of Forensic Psychology (ABFP)
www.abfp.com/

The American Academy of Forensic Psychology is approved by the American Psychological Association to offer continuing education for psychologists. The American Board of Forensic Psychology accredits these programs.

American Academy of Psychiatry and the Law (AAPL)
One Regency Drive
P.O. Box 30
Bloomfield, CT 06002
www.cc.emory.edu/AAPL/org.htm

The American Academy of Psychiatry and the Law is an organization of psychiatrists dedicated to excellence in practice, teaching, and research in forensic psychiatry.

American Association of Psychotherapists, Inc.
P.O. Box 140182
Dallas, TX 75214
aapinc.bigstep.com/

A professional association of licensed mental health clinicians.

American Psychiatric Association
1400 K Street NW
Washington, DC 20005
www.psych.org/main.html

The American Psychiatric Association is a medical specialty society whose physicians specialize in the diagnosis and treatment of mental and emotional illnesses and substance use disorders.

American Psychological Association (APA)
750 First Street NE
Washington, DC 20002-4242
www.apa.org

The American Psychological Association is the largest scientific and professional organization respresenting psychology in the United States and worldwide.

SOCIAL WORK AND MENTAL HEALTH COUNSELING

American Association of State Social Work Boards
400 South Ridge Parkway, Suite B
Culpeper, VA 22701
www.aasswb.org

American Counseling Association
5999 Stevenson Avenue
Alexandria, VA 22304-3300
www.counseling.org

For general information about counseling, as well as information on specialties such as school, college, mental health, rehabilitation, multicultural, career, marriage and family, and gerontological counseling.

Commission on Rehabilitation Counselor Certification
1835 Rolling Meadows Road, Suite E
Rolling Meadows, IL 60008

Council for Social Work Education
1700 Duke Street, Suite 500
Alexandria, VA 22314
www.cswe.org

Provides an annual directory of accredited B.S.W. and M.S.W. programs.

National Association of Social Workers
Career Information
750 First Street NE, Suite 700
Washington, DC 20002-4241

National Board for Certified Counselors, Inc.
3 Terrace Way, Suite D
Greensboro, NC 27403-3660
www.nbcc.org

FORENSIC COMPUTER INVESTIGATION

High Tech Crime Investigation Association
P.O. Box 4715
Rock Hill, SC 29732
www.charweb.org/organizations/clubs/pcg/htcia.htm

FORENSIC ECONOMICS

National Association of Forensic Economics (NAFE)
P.O. Box 30067
Kansas City, MO 64112
http://nafe.net/

APPENDIX B

FURTHER READING

JOURNALS

Forensic Science Communications

International Journal of Forensic Computing

Journal of the American Society of Questioned Document Examiners

Journal of Forensic Sciences

PSYCHOLOGY AND THE LAW

The following books are published by the American Psychological Association. For full book descriptions and ordering information, visit the APA website at www.apa.org.

Career Paths in Psychology: Where Your Degree Can Take You, by Robert J. Sternberg, 1997.

Dissertations and Theses from Start to Finish: Psychology and Related Fields, by John D. Cone and Sharon L. Foster, 1993.

Encyclopedia of Psychology: 8 Volume Set, by Alan E. Kazdin, Ph.D., Editor-in-Chief, 2000. Definitive guide to every area of psychological theory, research, and practice.

The Expert Expert Witness: More Maxims and Guidelines for Testifying in Court, by Stanley L. Brodsky, 1999. A practical and entertaining book for forensic psychologists.

Getting In: A Step-by-Step Plan for Gaining Admission to Graduate School in Psychology, 1993.

Graduate Study in Psychology: 2000 Edition, by Martha Braswell, 2000. Print and electronic versions. Offers practical information about more than five hundred psychology programs in the United States and Canada.

Law and Mental Health Professional Series. Help make your way through the labyrinth of state mental health law with these books from APA's Law and Mental Health Professionals series.

VGM Career Books

Camenson, Blythe. *On the Job: Real People Working in the Helping Professions*. Lincolnwood, IL: NTC/Contemporary, 1997.

DeGalan, Julie and Stephen Lambert. *Great Jobs for Psychology Majors*. Lincolnwood IL: NTC/Contemporary, 1995.

FORENSIC SCIENCE

Drug Enforcement Administration. *Basic Training Program for Drug Chemists*. DEA Office of Science and Technology, U.S. Dept. of Justice.

Lambert, Stephen and Debra Regan. *Great Jobs for Criminal Justice Majors.* Lincolnwood, IL: NTC/Contemporary, 2000.

Mills, Terry and Conrad Robertson. *Instrumental Data for Drug Analysis.* 2nd Ed. Boca Raton, FL: CRC Press, 1993.

Saferstein, Richard. *Criminalistics: An Introduction to Forensic Science*. Englewood Cliffs, NJ: Prentice Hall, 1990 (4th and previous editions are all applicable).

ACCIDENT INVESTIGATION

Traffic Accident Investigation Manual, Northwestern University.

www.northwestern.edu/nucps/index.htm

ANTHROPOLOGY

Haglund, William. "Beyond Bare Bones: Recent Developments in Forensic Anthropology." *Practicing Anthropology* 15(3):17–19.

Maples, Dr. William R. *Dead Men Do Tell Tales.* New York: Doubleday, 1994.

FORENSIC NURSING

Scope and Standards of Forensic Nursing Practice. Waldorf, MD: American Nurses Publishing.

www.nursingworld.org/ajn/1998/feb/anarsrc.htm

COMPUTER CRIME

Icove, David, Karl Seger and William Von Storch. *Computer Crime: A Crime Fighters Handbook.* Cambridge, MA: O'Reilly & Associates, 1995.

Rosenblatt, Ken. *High-Technology Crime: Investigating Cases Involving Computers.* San Jose, CA: KSK Publications, 1995.

APPENDIX C

FORENSIC LABORATORIES AND INSTITUTES

A quick search on the Internet will pull up these labs and institutes, as well as many others.

Alcohol, Tobacco and Firearms (ATF)

Arkansas State Crime Laboratory

The Armed Forces DNA Identification Laboratory (AFDIL)

Armed Forces Institute of Pathology

Bureau of Forensic Sciences—California Department of Justice

California Criminalistics Institute (CCI), Dept. of Justice, CA

Criminalistics Laboratory, Division of Criminal Investigation, Iowa State

Delaware State Police Crime Lab

Federal Bureau of Investigation

Food and Drug Administration's Forensic Center

Forensic News from Iowa

Forensic Science Agency of Northern Ireland

Forensic Science Center, Lawrence Livermore National Laboratory (LLNL)

Forensic Science Service

Hong Kong Government Forensic Laboratory

Institute of Science and Forensic Medicine (ISFM) Singapore

International Forensic Research Institute—Miami

Internet Pathology Laboratory, Justice Information Center

Laboratory of Pathology/NCI/NIH

Law Enforcement Medical Services

Metro-Dade (Miami) Police Department Crime Lab

Michigan State Police Forensic Science Division

National Center for Forensic Science (NCFS)

National Forensic Science Technology Center

National Institute of Justice (NIJ)

National Research Institute of Police Science—Japan

National Security Agency (NSA)

The Naval Criminal Investigative Service

RCMP Forensic Laboratory, Regina

Sacramento County Laboratory of Forensic Services

Uniformed Services University (USUHS) Department of Pathology

United States Army Criminal Investigation Laboratory

The United States Secret Service, Virginia Division of Forensic Science

U.S. Fish & Wildlife Services Forensic Laboratory

U.S. Postal Inspection Service

APPENDIX D

TRAINING PROGRAMS

The following is a list of colleges and universities that offer forensic science, forensic odontology, forensic psychology/law, forensic nursing, and forensic anthropology programs. Contact the individual schools for more information.

FORENSIC SCIENCE UNDERGRADUATE PROGRAMS

Albany State University
Criminal Justice Department/Forensic Science
504 College Drive
Albany, GA 31705
www.asurams.edu

College of Pennsylvania
Department of Chemistry
Country Club Road
York, PA 17045-7199
www.ycp.edu

Eastern Kentucky University
Department of Chemistry
337 Moore Building
521 Lancaster Avenue
Richmond, KY 40475-3102
www.eku.edu

Florida International University
Department of Chemistry
Miami, FL 33199
www.fiu.edu/~ifri/

Grossmont Community College
8800 Grossmont College Drive
El Cajon, CA 92020
http://grossmont.gcccd.cc.ca.us/aoj/aoj.htm

Jacksonville State University
College of Criminal Justice
Jacksonville, AL 36265-9982
www.jsu.edu

John Jay College of Criminal Justice
445 West 59th Street
New York, NY 10019
www.jjay.cuny.edu

Metropolitan State College
Department of Chemistry
P.O. Box 173362
Campus Box 52
Denver, CO 80217-3362
www.mscd.edu

Michigan State University
560 Baker Hall
East Lansing, MI 48824
www.msu.edu

National University
Forensic Science Program
11255 North Torrey Pines Road
La Jolla, CA 92037
www.nu.edu

Ohio University
Department of Chemistry
Clippinger Laboratory
Athens, OH 45701-2979
www.ohiou.edu

St. John's University
St. Vincent's College
8000 Utopia Parkway
Bent Room 268
Jamaica, NY 11439
www.stjohns.edu

University of Alabama at Birmingham
Department of Justice Science
University Station
901 South 15th Street
Birmingham, AL 35294-2060
www.uab.edu

University of Central Florida
Department of Chemistry
P.O. Box 162366
Orlando, FL 32816-2366
www.ucf.edu

University of Central Oklahoma
Department of Chemistry
100 North University Drive
Edmond, OK 73034
www.ucok.edu

University of Mississippi
Department of Chemistry
University, MS 38677
www.olemiss.edu

University of New Haven
Forensic Science Program
300 Orange Avenue
West Haven, CT 06516
www.newhaven.edu

The University of Southern Mississippi
Department of Polymer Science
Southern Station
Box 10076
Hattiesburg, MS 39406-0076
www.usm.edu

University of Tennessee—Knoxville
Forensic Anthropology Program
250 South Stadium Hall
Knoxville, TN 37996-0760
www.utk.edu

Vermont College of Norwich University
36 College Street
Montpelier, VT 05602
www.investigativepsych.com/madegree.htm

Virginia Commonwealth University
816 West Franklin Avenue
Richmond, VA 23284
www.vcu.edu

Weber State University
1137 University Circle
Ogden, UT 84407-1137
www.weber.edu

West Chester University
Department of Chemistry
West Chester, PA 19383
www.wcupa.edu

Canada

Laurentian University
Department of Biology
935 Ramsey Lake Road
Sudbury, Ontario
Canada P3E 2C6
www.laurentian.ca

University of Toronto at Mississauga
Forensic Science, Room 227
3359 Mississauga Road N.
Canada L5L 1C6
www.erin.utoronto.ca/academic/FSC/index.html

FORENSIC SCIENCE GRADUATE PROGRAMS

California State University, Los Angeles
Department of Criminal Justice
5151 State University Drive
Los Angeles, CA 90032-8163
www.calstatela.edu

California State University, Sacramento
School of Health and Human Services
Division of Criminal Justice
6000 J Street
Sacramento, CA 95819-6085
www.csus.edu

Florida International University
Department of Chemistry
Miami, FL 33199
www.fiu.edu/~ifri/Masters.html

George Washington University
Samson Hall 101
Department of Forensic Science
2036 H Street NW
Washington, DC 20052
www.gwu.edu/~forensic

George Washington University
Samson Hall 101
Department of Forensic Science
2036 H Street NW
Washington, DC 20052
www.gwu.edu/~forensic

John Jay College of Criminal Justice
445 West 59th Street
New York, NY 10019
www.jjay.cuny.edu

Marshall University School of Medicine
Office of Research and Graduate Education
1542 Spring Valley Drive
Huntington, WV 25755-9310
http://musom.marshall.edu/forensic

Michigan State University
560 Baker Hall
East Lansing, MI 48824-1118
www.msu.edu

National University
Forensic Science Program
11255 North Torrey Pines Road
La Jolla, CA 92037
www.NU.EDU

Southeast Missouri State University
1 University Plaza
Cape Girardeau, MO 63701
www.semo.edu

University of Alabama at Birmingham
Department of Justice Science
University Station
901 South 15th Street
Birmingham, AL 35294-2060
www.uab.edu

University of Central Oklahoma
Department of Chemistry
100 North University Drive
Edmond, OK 73034
www.chemistry.ucok.edu/Masters.htm

University of Florida
Distance Education in Forensic Science
Department of Physiological Studies
http://grove.ufl.edu/~forensic/

University of Illinois at Chicago
Forensic Science Program MC866
833 South Wood Street
Chicago, IL 60612-2250
www.uic.edu/pharmacy/depts/forensicsci/

University of New Haven
Forensic Science Program
300 Orange Avenue
West Haven, CT 06516
www.newhaven.edu

University of North Texas Health Science Center at Fort Worth
Graduate School of Biomedical Sciences
3500 Camp Bowie Boulevard
Fort Worth, TX 76107-2699
www.hsc.unt.edu

Virginia Commonwealth University
816 West Franklin Avenue
Richmond, VA 23284
www.vcu.edu

Wayne State University
Department of Mortuary Service
Division of Forensic Science
5439 Woodard
Detroit, MI 48202
www.mortuarysciencewayne.org

West Chester University
Department of Chemistry
West Chester, PA 19383
www.wcupa.edu

FORENSIC SCIENCE DOCTORAL PROGRAMS

At this time, the American Academy of Forensic Sciences (AAFS) does not have information on active doctoral programs in forensic science in the United States. There are, though, several universities offering doctoral programs with some specialization relating to forensic science. These are as follows:

University of Alabama at Birmingham
Department of Justice Science
University Station
901 South 15th Street
Birmingham, AL 35294-2060
www.uab.edu

John Jay College of Criminal Justice
445 West 59th Street
New York, NY 10019
www.jjay.cuny.edu

Ohio University
Department of Chemistry
Clippinger Laboratories
Athens, OH 45701

University of California, Berkeley
140 Warren Hall
Berkeley, CA 94720
www.berkeley.edu

University of Illinois at Chicago
Forensic Science Program MC866
833 South Wood Street
Chicago, IL 60612-2250
www.uic.edu

There are also a number of universities that offer research emphasis in forensic science as shown in recent theses that were forensic-related.

University of Alabama
Department of Chemistry
Box 870336
Tuscaloosa, AL 35487-0336
www.ua.edu

Kansas State University
Department of Chemistry
Willard Hall
Manhattan, KS 66506
www.ksu.edu

Villanova University
Department of Chemistry
800 Lancaster Avenue
Villanova, PA 19085
www.villanova.edu

University of Virginia
Department of Chemistry
McCormick Road, Room 234
Charlottesville, VA 22903
www.uva.edu

UNDERGRADUATE AND GRADUATE COURSES IN FORENSIC ODONTOLOGY

Louisiana State University
1100 Florida Avenue/Box 142
New Orleans, LA 70119-2799
www.lsusd.lsumd.edu

Northwestern University
Health Science Building
240 East Huron
Chicago, IL 60611

University of Louisville School of Dentistry
Surgical and Hospital Dentistry
501 South Preston Street
Louisville, KY 40202
www.dental.louisville.edu

University of Texas
Dental Branch
Houston, TX 77225

Approved Courses in Forensic Odontology

American Board of Forensic Odontology (ABFO)
The Forensic Sciences Foundation
P.O. Box 669
Colorado Springs, CO 80901-0669
www.abfo.org

The Armed Forces Institute of Pathology
Center for Advanced Medical Education
6825 16th Street NW
Washington, DC 20306
www.afip.org
(one-week course every March)

University of Texas Health Science Center at San Antonio, Dental School
Department of Dental Diagnostic Science
7703 Floyd Curl Drive
San Antonio, TX 78284
(week-long program offered every other year)

GRADUATE PROGRAMS IN PSYCHOLOGY AND LAW

University of Alabama

Allegheny University of the Health Sciences/Villanova University

University of Arizona

California Professional School of Psychology—Fresno

Castleton State College

University of Denver

Florida International University

Illinois School of Professional Psychology/Chicago

University of Illinois at Chicago

John Jay College

University of Minnesota

University of Nebraska

Nova Southeastern University

The Sage Colleges

Sam Houston State University

Simon Fraser University

FORENSIC NURSING—UNDERGRADUATE PROGRAMS

What follows is a brief listing of forensic nursing courses or programs. Visit www.forensiceducation.com/eduinternational.htm for updated information.

B.A. in Forensic Health Care Studies Affiliation
Sheffield Hallam University
Ashworth Hospital
Liverpool, England
www.nhsconfed.net/ashworth/ashcentr.htm

St. George's Hospital Medical School
Section of Forensic Psychiatry, London, UK
Multi-Disciplinary Diploma in Forensic Mental Health
http://infoserv.sghms.ac.uk/

FORENSIC NURSING—MASTER'S DEGREE

Fitchburg State College
Fitchburg, MA
www.fsc.edu/www/index.html
www.fsc.edu/www/academics_graduate_course_nursing.html

University of Western Sydney
Macarthur, Campbelltown NSW
Australia
http://fohweb.macarthur.uws.edu.au/ceec/courses/forensic.htm

FORENSIC NURSING COURSES

Forensic Medicine for Nurses, CPD Course
Department of Forensic Medicine
University of Dundee
Dundee, Scotland, DD1 4HN
www.dundee.ac.uk/forensicmedicine/

The University of Calgary
www.ucalgary.ca
www.nursing.ucalgary.ca/

Forensic Health Studies
Mount Royal College
Calgary, Alberta
Canada
www.mtroyal.ab.ca/programs/centrehs/forensic/

Rutgers University
New Brunswick, NJ
Correctional Nursing Course
www.rutgers.edu/

The University of Texas at Austin
School of Nursing Continuing Education Program
Courses in forensic nursing
www.utexas.edu/index.html

The University of Colorado—Bethel College,
Forensic Nursing
Colorado Springs, CO
www.uccs.edu/

Legal Nurse Consulting Programs
The NACLNC-Medical-Legal Consulting Institute, Inc.
www.legalnurse.com

Sexual Assault Nurse Examiner
American Forensic Nurses
Distance Education Programs
www.amrn.com/

Forensic Nursing Services Online
SART/SANE courses
www.forensicnursing.com

Sexual Assault Nurse Examiner Program
www.state.ky.us/agencies/gov/sane.htm

Connecticut Sexual Assault Crisis Services
www.connsacs.org/GBS.htm

Rutgers University
New Brunswick, NJ
Sexual Assault Examiner Course
www.rutgers.edu/

Nursing and Death Investigation
Dade County
Miami, FL
www.thename.org/NODIA/NODIANurs.htm

FORENSIC ANTHROPOLOGY

Please note that this is not an exhaustive list of all of the schools offering courses in forensic anthropology; check the Anthropology Association Guide to Departments for a more comprehensive listing.

Undergraduate Programs in Anthropology with Forensic Anthropology Faculty:

California State, Chico

University of California, Santa Cruz

University of Indianapolis, Indiana

University of North Carolina at Charlotte

University of North Carolina at Wilmington

University of Tennessee—Knoxville

Post-Baccalaureate Advanced Certificate in Forensic Anthropology (Post-Bac means after the B.A./B.S. degree, but not a graduate degree):

Mercyhurst College, Erie, PA

Graduate Programs in Anthropology with Forensic Anthropology Faculty:

Louisiana State University

State University of New York (SUNY)—Binghampton

University of Florida, Gainesville

University of Illinois, Urbana-Champaign

University of South Carolina, Columbia

University of Tennesee, Knoxville

Western Michigan University, Kalamazoo

Wichita State University, Kansas